JEWISH HOLY DAYS

THEIR PROPHETIC AND CHRISTIAN SIGNIFICANCE

Coulson Shepherd

LOIZEAUX BROTHERS
Neptune, New Jersey

FOURTH EDITION, JANUARY 1977
EIGHTH PRINTING, MARCH 1988

Published 1961 by LOIZEAUX BROTHERS, Inc.

*A Nonprofit Organization, Devoted to the Lord's Work
and to the Spread of His Truth*

Library of Congress Catalog Card Number: 61-16660

ISBN 0-87213-780-5

PRINTED IN THE UNITED STATES OF AMERICA

To EDITH

My Beloved Wife

who helped in the preparation of these messages
and who has been the greatest earthly help to me
for almost half a century

THIS BOOK IS AFFECTIONATELY DEDICATED

CONTENTS

FOREWORD

Holidays!

WHO DOESN'T like holidays? They come to us out of our childhood, freighted with the sweet and tender memories of family and home. They have been the occasion of so many delightful experiences in the years since childhood. A kaleidoscope of dear familiar faces of family and friends passes before memory's eyes, and there is the sensation of the heavy perfume of loving words and kindly deeds. All the homespun virtues of our American way of life add special significance to these precious things from the storehouse of the past. We stand in solemn awe before the sacrifice and devotion which purchased some of these days for us and made possible our cherished freedoms. We resent the desecration of these days by the greedy encroachment of commercialism.

But great as are our beloved holidays, their origin is from men. How different are Israel's holy days, as holidays should be pronounced if we would get the original thought behind the word! No other nation ever had *God* establish their holidays, as did Israel, while waiting—supernaturally sustained in the wilderness—to enter the Promised Land. Each of these holy days spoke of God's concern and care for His people. In the case of those added later, such as Purim and Hanukkah, men established them in the fear of God in gratefulness for God's gracious intervention in human affairs for their deliverance. How thrilling to have days like these to celebrate.

7

Jewish Holy Days

Too many Christians are illiterate of the meaning and significance of these great days in the history and life of their Jewish friends. I know of no one better qualified than Coulson Shepherd, an alumnus of our college and friend and brother of both Jew and Christian, to tell of these great days and their spiritual significance. It has been my privilege to talk intimately of these things with him and to hear him speak so warmly of his friends who keep these days, sometimes unwittingly of their scriptural greatness and message. My heart has been warmed . . . and so will yours be as you read this book!

Clarence E. Mason, Jr.

PREFACE

(If Preface is read, the following chapters
will be better understood.)

THE holidays in Jewry are not only historic, but prophetic and very definitely point to Israel's Messiah. "These are the feasts of the Lord, even holy convocations, which ye shall proclaim in their seasons" (Leviticus 23:4).

In addition to these seven Feasts of Jehovah, other days were added in later years to commemorate certain events. But according to the original Levitical instructions there were only seven occasions during the year when Israel was to observe religious festivals and fasts. To take in other important holidays in Jewry, we have included Purim, Independence Day, Hanukkah, and Christmas, which is really Jewish.

The seven Feasts of Jehovah are arranged in Leviticus 23 in two groups. The first four came at the beginning of the Biblical Jewish year, while the last three came toward the end

9

of the year. That seems to be God's method in revealing future things (compare Luke 1:31-33). Between these two groups there was a period of several months, when there were no feasts or holy convocations. The Feasts of Passover and Unleavened Bread point to Christ's death and burial; Firstfruits to His resurrection; and Pentecost (fifty days later) to His Church. Then there is the space of time representing the long period in which Israel is out of the Land of Promise and out of the place of blessing, which coincides with the Church Age. Finally, there are the last three—Feast of Trumpets, Day of Atonement, and Feast of Tabernacles—all of which foreshadow the next prophetic events, namely, the Regathering of Israel and Rapture of the Church, the Time of Jacob's Trouble and his ultimate salvation, and the Kingdom Age, respectively.

The first of the Feasts is Passover and is found in the beginning of the Old Testament. It points very definitely to our Lord's sacrificial death. The last one is the Feast of Tabernacles, the fulfillment of which is recorded at the end of the Old Testament, namely, Zechariah 14:16-21, which is a picture of the millennium.

Truly, "coming events cast their shadows before." These seven Feasts of Jehovah "are a shadow of things to come" (Colossians 2:17). "Now all these things happened unto them for ensamples [as types]: and they are written for our admonition, upon whom the ends of the world [age] are come" (1 Corinthians 10:11).

The New Testament is the only *divine* commentary on the Old Testament. As has oft been quoted:

> The New is in the Old contained;
> The Old is by the New explained.

In our broadcasts these messages were addressed primarily to those "Who are Israelites; to whom pertaineth the adoption, and the glory, and the covenants, and the giving of the law, and the service of God, and the promises; Whose are the fathers, and of whom as concerning the flesh Christ came, who is over all, God blessed for ever" (Romans 9:4-5).

However, they are applicable to all. While the Nation of Israel is different and distinct from all other nations, there is no difference when it comes to individual Jews and Gentiles. There is no difference respecting sin (Romans 3:9-23), and there is no difference when it comes to salvation (Romans 10:12-13).

It is interesting to note the meaning of the Hebrew word translated "feast." The root idea of the word carries the thought of "to keep an appointment." God made appointments with His covenant people to meet with them at certain times. He told them to come to Him and gave the exact days when they should come and how these special days were to be observed. When we, Jews or Gentiles, keep our appointment with God, we really feast with Him. When these feasts are observed without the Lord they become "the feasts of the Jews" and not the feasts of the Lord (John 6:4).

It should be noted that we list on page 14 the Jewish Holidays during the next ten-year period according to the Jewish calendar, but we have arranged our messages according to the Gregorian calendar. The Jewish New Year is nowhere to be found in Scripture and neither is there any ground to substitute it for the Feast of Trumpets.

Grateful acknowledgment is given to Keith L. Brooks, Victor Buksbazen, Sidney J. Clarke, Joseph Hoffman Cohen, M. R. De Haan, Edward Drew, Lily Edelman, Charles Feinberg, Aaron Judah Kligerman, William L. Pettingill, and Israel Sax. Books and articles from their pens were most helpful through the years in preparing these messages.

This book is sent forth with the prayer that it will help Jewish people to see their Messiah, Jeshua Hamashiah, and be visited with His great salvation. Also, that Gentiles will see the wonders of divine revelation and believe to the saving of their souls. It is also our prayer that it will prove a rich blessing to Christians. It should be the means of creating better understanding and more friendly relations between Jews and Christians from a scriptural standpoint. Such demonstrated knowledge on the part of Christians will help them to be a spiritual blessing especially to Jewish people.

C. S.

Patchogue, Long Island, New York

Calendar of JEWISH HOLY DAYS

Holy Days	1984	1985	1986	1987	1988	1989	1990	1991	1992	1993	1994	1995	1996	1997	1998
New Year of Trees Shebat 15	Jan. 19	Feb. 6	Jan. 25	Feb. 14	Feb. 3	Jan. 21	Feb. 10	Jan. 30	Jan. 20	Feb. 6	Jan. 27	Jan. 16	Feb. 5	Jan. 23	Feb. 11
Purim First Adar 14*		Mar. 7		Mar. 14	Mar. 2		Mar. 10	Feb. 27		Mar. 7	Feb. 25		Mar. 5		Mar. 12
Purim Second Adar 14*	Mar. 18		Mar. 25			Mar. 21			Mar. 19			Mar. 16		Mar. 23	
Passover Nisan 15**	Apr. 17	Apr. 6	Apr. 24	Apr. 14	Apr. 2	Apr. 20	Apr. 10	Mar. 30	Apr. 18	Apr. 6	Mar. 27	Apr. 15	Apr. 4	Apr. 22	Apr. 11
Independence Day Iyar 5	May 7	Apr. 26	May 14	May 4	Apr. 22	May 10	Apr. 30	Apr. 19	May 8	Apr. 26	Apr. 16	May 5	Apr. 24	May 12	May 1
Lag B'Omer Iyar 18	May 20	May 9	May 27	May 17	May 5	May 23	May 13	May 2	May 21	May 9	Apr. 29	May 18	May 7	May 25	May 14
Shabuoth Shivan 6*	June 6	May 26	June 13	June 3	May 22	June 9	May 30	May 19	June 7	May 26	May 16	June 4	May 24	June 11	May 3
Tisha B'Av Av 9	Aug. 7	July 28	Aug. 14	Aug. 4	July 24	Aug. 10	July 31	July 21	Aug. 9	July 27	July 17	Aug. 6	July 25	Aug. 12	Aug. 2
Rosh Hashanah Tishri 1*	Sept. 27	Sept. 16	Oct. 4	Sept. 24	Sept. 12	Sept. 30	Sept. 20	Sept. 9	Sept. 28	Sept. 16	Sept. 6	Sept. 25	Sept. 14	Oct. 2	Sept. 21
Yom Kippur Tishri 10	Oct. 6	Sept. 25	Oct. 13	Oct. 3	Sept. 21	Oct. 9	Sept. 29	Sept. 18	Oct. 7	Sept. 25	Sept. 15	Oct. 4	Sept. 23	Oct. 11	Sept. 30
Succoth Tishri 15-22	Oct. 11	Sept. 30	Oct. 18	Oct. 8	Sept. 26	Oct. 14	Oct. 4	Sept. 23	Oct. 12	Sept. 30	Sept. 20	Oct. 9	Sept. 28	Oct. 16	Oct. 5
Simhat Torah Tishri 23	Oct. 19	Oct. 8	Oct. 26	Oct. 16	Oct. 4	Oct. 22	Oct. 12	Oct. 1	Oct. 20	Oct. 8	Sept. 28	Oct. 17	Oct. 6	Oct. 24	Oct. 13
Hanukkah Kislev 25**	Dec. 19	Dec. 8	Dec. 27	Dec. 16	Dec. 4	Dec. 23	Dec. 12	Dec. 2	Dec. 20	Dec. 9	Nov. 28	Dec. 18	Dec. 6	Dec. 24	Dec. 14

Note: The Jewish Holy Days begin the evening before at sundown.
     Celebrated the following day also.
     Celebrated the following seven days also.
Firstfruits had not been observed in Jewry for over 2,000 years. However, since the State of Israel has been established, it is being observed in Israel. Because of the difference in the Jewish and Gregorian calendars, only occasionally does the date correspond with Easter. It is always "on the morrow after the Sabbath," a Sunday, the day Christ arose.

CHRONOLOGY OF JEWISH CALENDAR

THE JEWISH YEARS are counted according to the World Era, beginning with the creation of man according to Biblical chronology. Hence year One started with Adam. The World Era came into general use only during the tenth or eleventh century. Before that time, various eras were used in documents. The Bible counts years either from the Exodus from Egypt, or the years of reigning kings. When the Temple was destroyed another chronology was begun from that date. This continued until the present reckoning of time.

The political rebirth of the State of Israel has rekindled in Jewish minds the establishment of a new Sanhedrin that will be recognized by the whole people of Israel. One task of that august body will be to consider suggestions that have been made for a new chronology to be dated from the capture of Jerusalem by General Edmund H. H. Allenby in 1917 during World War I; or perhaps to have the new reckoning date from May 14, 1948, the date of the establishment of the State of Israel.

Because of the aversion to counting time from the birth of Christ, Jewish people indicate the years before Him as B.C.E. (Before Common Era); and the years following His birth as C.E. (Common Era).

PURIM

Feast of Esther

ACCORDING TO THE GREGORIAN CALENDAR, Purim is the
first important holiday in Jewry, but it occurs in the twelfth
month in the Jewish Biblical year. This is one of the very happy
festive commemorations among the Jewish people. It is not
one of the Feasts of Jehovah commanded to be kept in Leviticus 23, but the Scripture does teach that the Jewish people
should "keep these two days . . . and that these days should
be remembered and kept throughout every generation" (Esther
9:27, 28). So, year after year on the fourteenth and fifteenth
of Adar* (in leap year, II Adar) the sons of Jacob commemorate their deliverance from destruction in Persia about twenty-
four hundred years ago.

A Thrilling True Story

In synagogues the Megillah, the book of Esther, is read.
And what a thrilling story this book contains! Read about
Esther, a Jewish maiden who was chosen by King Ahasuerus
as his queen because of her great natural beauty. Mordecai, her
cousin, will command your respect and admiration as you behold him standing for his convictions against great odds. There
is not only a beautiful queen as heroine, a brave and pious
Mordecai, but there is a villain as fiendish and as cruel as Hitler and his henchmen of our day. This Haman, the prime min-
ister of Persia, planned the extermination of all Jews and

---

*The Jewish month Adar invariably corresponds with March.

17

erected a gallows upon which Mordecai was to die.

The name of God is not found in the book, but in no book of the Bible is the presence of God more manifest, especially in protecting and preserving His covenant people, Israel. God turned the tables as He did in the case of Hitler, Streicher, Goering, Himmler, Eichmann, and company of Nazi Germany; and Haman, with his ten sons, died on the gallows intended for Mordecai. This is all an evidence that "He that keepeth Israel shall neither slumber nor sleep" (Psalm 121:4.)

It was Haman who really named the holiday, although he did not mean to do so. Eager to choose the best day to carry out his fiendish plans, and being superstitious, he threw lots, a kind of dice, called in Hebrew, Pur. The numbers on the Purim were 13 and 12, which he believed to mean the thirteenth day of the twelfth month, Adar (Esther 3:7, 12). So he commanded that his wicked order of Jewish extermination be carried out on that day.

When the Megillah is read in the synagogues on this happy holiday, at times and in some places, Jewish children protest against Haman's wickedness by shaking rattles and stamping feet whenever his name is mentioned. Purim is considered by many as the very best day in the Jewish calendar year. They even have a proverb, "Not every day is Purim!" But every day can be Purim for every Jew who will heed this message.

To try to destroy all the Jews is like a little fish trying to drink up all the water in the vast Pacific, or a puny midget trying to kick over the Rock of Gibraltar.

The Only Indestructible Nation

In an encyclopedia published in Germany during Hitler's heydey, it is declared, "In less than one hundred years the Jewish problem will be solved. The race will simply have disappeared." The writer of that prediction might profitably have made a trip to Cairo before using his would-be prophetic pen. There in Cairo he could have found food for thought by reading on a slab of granite these words of Rameses II, written three thousand years ago: "Israel is annihilated; Israel will have no posterity!" Rameses II is gone; Haman with his entire posterity is gone; Hitler and his henchmen are gone; but Israel will never cease to exist as a nation. Here is one nation that God said shall never perish from the earth!

History often repeats itself, and I wonder why we are so slow to learn from the lessons of the past. As our Jewish friends read the book of Esther, we wish they would do so not so much as a form or matter of ceremony, but really study the record of their deliverance from the murderous hands of Haman, as it is so thrillingly given in the Megillah, the scroll that is read on the fourteenth of Adar. This record should give us a clue as to what our course of conduct should be in the present Middle East crisis, and in all our troubles and problems when the world is still filled with people tarred with the same stick as Haman and Hitler.

The key to the story of deliverance in the days of Ahasuerus, is found in the fourth chapter of the book of Esther. When Mordecai, Queen Esther's cousin, learned that the decree had gone forth "to destroy, to kill, and to cause to perish, all Jews, both young and old, little children and women" (Esther 3:13), he "rent his clothes, and . . . there was great mourning among the Jews, and fasting, and weeping, and wailing; and many lay in sackcloth and ashes" (Esther 4: 1, 2). Mordecai sent word to Queen Esther informing her "of all that had happened . . . and of the sum of money that Haman had promised to pay to the king's treasuries for the Jews, to destroy them" (Esther 4:7). He charged her to "go in unto the king, to make supplication unto him, and to make request before him for her people" (4:8). Esther then sent out word to Mordecai, saying: "All of the king's servants, and the people of the king's provinces, do know, that whosoever, whether man or woman, shall come unto the king into the inner court, who is not called, there is one law of his to put

19

him to death, except such to whom the king shall hold out the golden sceptre, that he may live: but I have not been called to come in unto the king these thirty days. And they told to Mordecai Esther's words.

"Then Mordecai commanded to answer Esther, Think not with thyself that thou shalt escape in the king's house, more than all the Jews. For if thou altogether holdest thy peace at this time, then shall there enlargement and deliverance arise to the Jews from another place; but thou and thy father's house shall be destroyed: and who knoweth whether thou art come to the kingdom for such a time as this?

"Then Esther bade them return to Mordecai this answer, Go, gather together all the Jews that are present in Shushan, and fast ye for me, and neither eat nor drink three days, night or day: I also and my maidens will fast likewise; and so will I go in unto the king, which is not according to the law: and if I perish, I perish. So Mordecai went his way, and did according to all that Esther had commanded him" (Esther 3:11-17).

The Golden Scepter

Do you remember the Hebrew name for Esther? It is *Hadassah* (Esther 2:7). Today we have a world-wide organization of fine Jewish women known as *Hadassah*. If only the members of Hadassah would become Queen Esthers in the sense that, at the risk of their lives, they would seek the face of God! If they would only go to Him, pointing to the scepter that will gain an audience with Him, the King of kings. If these twentieth-century Hadassahs, and all Jewish people, only knew that the *Golden Scepter* at the right hand of their God is held out to them, they would go in unto the King, and make supplication to Him, and make request before Him.

It is a foregone conclusion that when the Jews in the days of Ahasuerus fasted three days and nights, that fasting was accompanied by repentance, affliction of soul, and earnest heart-breaking and heart-searching prayers to the God of Abraham, Isaac, and Jacob, to bring them deliverance.

Fast with me. . . . If the scepter had not been held out to Queen Esther, she would have perished. If there is no scepter held out to the Hadassahs of today, they too, will perish. But praise God, there is a Scepter. The Scepter is a Person. In Numbers, the fourth book of Moses, we read: "A Sceptre shall rise out of Israel" (Numbers 24:17).

That Scepter is the promised Messiah, who came nineteen hundred years ago and by the sacrifice of Himself provided complete redemption for all Hadassahs and all Jews and Gentiles. All who believe in Him and look to Him, can have an audience with God, who alone is able to deliver them from bloodthirsty Jew-hating Hamans of today and save them from their sins.

Just as Esther could not approach her king years ago, unless the golden scepter was held out to her, so today no person, Jew or Gentile, can approach God unless the Scepter, the Christ of God at His right hand, is held out. He says to all who have ears to hear: "I am the way, the truth, and the life: no man cometh unto the Father, but by Me" (John 14:6).

Millions of individual Jews and Gentiles have approached God in the name of the Messiah, Jeshua Hamashiah, the true Scepter of Righteousness (Psalm 45:6; Hebrews 1:8). They have approached God by Him, and know He is the cure for their sins and all troubles and problems. Will you trust Him at this Purim season? Esther said, "I will, and if I perish, I perish!" Will you—even at the risk of losing friends, relatives, and position—trust Him? Search your Scriptures and honestly consider Jeshua the Christ. As you really look to your God for light, you will come to believe that Jeshua is the Son of God, the Scepter, and the only approach to God; you will believe that He died for your sins on God's altar of sacrifice and rose again according to the Old Testament Scriptures (1 Corinthians 15:1-4).

The record tells us, Esther "required nothing" (Esther

2:15). Many people today, Jews and Gentiles, are prosperous. They have fine homes and good positions. The modern Hadassahs, like their beautiful predecessor, require nothing. They feel they have need of nothing. But, like Esther, all have need of deliverance.

Because of who the Scepter is—the Saviour-Messiah, the Eternal Son of God—and because of what He did—died as the Lamb of God for our sins and shed His precious blood—our God, the God of Abraham, Isaac, and Jacob, who is altogether holy, can now righteously forgive us our sins, if and when we believe in the Lord Jesus Christ as Saviour.

With a great Jewish scholar of a bygone day, I say: "I am not ashamed of the gospel of Christ: for it is the power of God unto salvation to every one that believeth; to the Jew first, and also to the Gentile. For therein [that is, within the facts of the gospel—Messiah's death and resurrection] is the righteousness of God revealed from faith to faith: as it is written [in Habakkuk 2:4], The just shall live by faith" (Romans 1:16-17).

To quote a great Scotsman, James McKendrick, "We are not swindled into Heaven, nor smuggled into glory; we are saved righteously."

"Wherefore He is able also to save them to the uttermost that come unto God *by Him,* seeing He ever liveth to make intercession for them" (Hebrews 7:25). This is God's way, and the only way of salvation. It is the only way of hanging the many Hamans of today, so that *every day can be Purim!*

PASSOVER

Festival of Freedom

PASSOVER IS ANOTHER HAPPY SEASON in Jewry. There is great preparation in Jewish homes for this Festival of Freedom. For several days Jewish people throughout the world cleanse their homes of all leaven in anticipation of celebrating Sedar. No matter what the circumstances, wherever a Jewish family still has a roof over its head and a box of matzoth, there mother and children gather around the table where father directs the traditional and time-hallowed ritual.

Here we have the first two of the seven Feasts of the Lord, described in the twenty-third chapter of Leviticus, namely, Passover and Feast of Unleavened Bread. These are combined today in the Passover and last seven days. Hence, the seven days observance in Jewry today. "These are the feasts of the Lord, even holy convocations, which ye shall proclaim in their seasons. In the fourteenth day of the first month* at even is the Lord's passover. And on the fifteenth day of the same month is the feast of unleavened bread unto the Lord: seven days ye must eat unleavened bread" (Leviticus 23:4-6).

---

*Known today as Nisan and so called in Esther 3:7. It is the first month of the Biblical year which begins with the new moon at the end of March. It is called Abib in Exodus 13:4; 34:18; Deuteronomy 16:1. Nisan corresponds with April, but sometimes takes in the latter part of March.

A Prophetic Picture of Events

The other five feasts are: Firstfruits, Pentecost, Trumpets, Atonement, and Tabernacles. These seven holy convocations are very significant prophetically. In this message and in subsequent ones we will see how each of these Feasts of Jehovah very vividly speaks of the person and work of the Messiah. The seven feasts of Leviticus 23 present a picture of the orderly chronology of events from Calvary to the millennium.

In this message, we are considering the first two: Passover and Unleavened Bread together because they are observed as one in Jewry.

The instructions for the original Passover are found in Exodus 12: "And the Lord spake unto Moses and Aaron in the land of Egypt, saying, This month shall be unto you the beginning of months: it shall be the first month of the year to you. Speak ye unto all the congregation of Israel, saying, In the tenth day of this month they shall take to them every man a lamb, according to the house of their fathers, a lamb for an house: And if the household be too little for the lamb, let him and his neighbour next unto his house take it according to the number of the souls; every man according to his eating shall make your count for the lamb. Your lamb shall be without blemish, a male of the first year: ye shall take it out from the sheep, or from the goats: And ye shall keep it up until the fourteenth day of the same month: and the whole assembly of the congregation of Israel shall kill it in the evening.

"And they shall take of the blood, and strike it on the two side posts and on the upper door post of the houses, wherein they shall eat it. And they shall eat the flesh in that night, roast with fire, and unleavened bread; and with bitter herbs they shall eat it. Eat not of it raw, nor sodden at all with water, but roast with fire; his head with his legs, and with the purtenance thereof. And ye shall let nothing of it remain until the morning; and that which remaineth of it until the morning ye shall burn with fire. And thus shall ye eat it; with your loins girded, your shoes on your feet, and your staff in your hand; and ye shall eat it in haste: it is the Lord's passover.

"For I will pass through the land of Egypt this night, and will smite all the firstborn in the land of Egypt, both man and beast; and against all the gods of Egypt I will execute judgment: I am the Lord. And the blood shall be to you for a token upon the houses where ye are: and when I see the blood, I will pass over you, and the plague shall not be upon you to destroy you, when I smite the land of Egypt.

"And this day shall be unto you for a memorial; and ye shall keep it a feast to the Lord throughout your generations; ye shall keep it a feast by an ordinance for ever. Seven days shall ye eat unleavened bread; even the first day ye shall put away leaven out of your houses: for whosoever eateth leavened bread from the first day until the seventh day, that soul shall be cut off from Israel."

Since that memorable night in Egypt 3,500 years ago, Jewish people have been observing annually that deliverance. Wonderfully and beautifully touching are the instructions given to Israel through Moses: "And when thy son asketh thee in time to come, saying, What mean the testimonies, and the statutes, and the judgments, which the Lord our God hath commanded you? Then thou shalt say unto thy son, We were Pharaoh's bondmen in Egypt; and the Lord brought us out of Egypt with a mighty hand: And the Lord showed signs and wonders, great and sore, upon Egypt, upon Pharaoh, and upon all his household, before our eyes: And He brought us out from thence, that He might bring us in, to give us the land which He sware unto our fathers" (Deuteronomy 6:20-23.)

Thus it developed down through the centuries that the Jewish boy seated at the Passover table would go through the ritual which involved asking the father certain questions. The boy asks, "Why is this night different from all other nights?" Then follows the recital by the father of all the wonderful events that led up to the Passover deliverance from the

Pharaohs. So there is kept alive, age after age, that racial cohesiveness which makes the Jewish people self-conscious and causes them to realize how, in many wonderful ways, God has accomplished His miraculous preservation.

That is the reason why Jewish people, even against hope, can press on, and know that all the Pharaohs, Hamans, Herods, and Hitlers together cannot wipe them out. If the nation of Israel can be wiped out, then God would be the greater loser, for His Word is at stake; He said they would never cease to exist as a nation. During those early days of Joseph's sojourn in Egypt, it looked as though the nation was doomed to go out of existence because of the famine and pestilence in the land. That small company, only about seventy-five souls, was preserved by going down into Egypt, but there they grew to six hundred thousand men, besides women and children.

In some places, perhaps even in Israel, it must seem that death is again stalking close to the Passover door. In such places I can imagine it is not safe to leave the door open—not even for Elijah! Rabbis of old taught that the Messiah was most likely to come on the night of Passover. A vacant chair is to be seen at the Sedar feast for Elijah, the herald of the Messiah (Malachi 4:5-6).

Next Year Jerusalem?

How wonderful that so many of our Jewish friends, from all parts of the world, can celebrate Passover in the land of their fathers. Millions living in Israel, and hundreds of thousands of tourists from the west, the north, the south, and the east, are in the land. The traditional, hopeful saying of the centuries, "Next year, Jerusalem!" cannot be said by them, for they are in Jerusalem.

The Saturday before Passover is Metzora-Shabbat Hagadol, the Great Sabbath. It commemorates the procuring of the Passover Lamb. In that original Metzora of long ago in Egypt, and the subsequent slaying of the lamb, being commemorated now, we recall how God heard the cry of the Jewish people. He knew their sorrows; He came down to deliver them by means of the shed and applied blood of the Passover Lamb. The Lord God still hears our cry; He knows our sorrows and has come down to deliver us. In the true meaning of Passover, people today—Jews and Gentiles—can learn how they can enjoy an eternal Festival of Freedom.

The Passover Table

Now let us look carefully at the table Jewish people will gather around. What will be on the table? There will be the shank bone of a sheep, unleavened bread, bitter herbs, wine, candles, an egg, salt water, greens, and grated apple. These things, admittedly are very significant; but God ordered only three things. Before I name the three things ordered by God, let us look at these items that will be on the Passover table. All agree that a bloodless shank bone of a sheep is a poor substitute for the prescribed Passover lamb. The bread must be unleavened for leaven is a type of evil. Bitter herbs look back to the bitter sufferings under the lash of Egyptian taskmasters. The wine speaks of sacrificial blood. The candles bring to our minds the Tabernacle worship in the wilderness. The egg is added because in it are the qualities of life, a type of resurrection. Salt water speaks of tears shed in Egypt. The grated apple, having the color of clay, recalls the clay with which bricks were made in that long ago. Yes, these things are very significant.

Let us consider in more detail the unleavened bread on the table, the three matzoth, for this also is the Feast of Unleavened Bread. The middle matzo is broken and half of it is hidden. The hidden half is brought forth and eaten by every member of the family at the end of the meal. It is called afikomen. Could these three matzoth be symbolic of the triunity of the God of Abraham, Isaac, and Jacob? Here on the Sedar table this truth is clearly symbolized. The middle matzo, the one that is broken, pictures the Messiah. We read that when

He sat down at the Passover table with His disciples, He took bread, broke it, and divided it among His disciples. He then said, *"Take, eat: this is My body, which is broken for you: this do in remembrance of Me"* (1 Corinthians 11:24). The broken and hidden half of the matzo is typical of His death and burial. And the bringing forth of it at the end of the meal is symbolic of His resurrection.

When the Messiah was on earth He kept the Passover with His Jewish followers, the disciples. "Now the first day of the feast of unleavened bread the disciples come to Jesus, saying unto Him, Where wilt Thou that we prepare for Thee to eat the passover? And He said, Go into the city to such a man, and say unto him, The Master saith, My time is at hand; I will keep the passover at thy house with My disciples. And the disciples did as Jesus had appointed them; and they made ready the passover. Now when the even was come, He sat down with the twelve. . . . And as they were eating, Jesus took bread, and blessed it, and brake it, and gave it to the disciples, and said, Take, eat; this is My body. And He took the cup, and gave thanks, and gave it to them, saying, Drink ye all of it; For this is My blood of the new testament, which is shed for many for the remissions of sins. But I say unto you, I will not drink henceforth of this fruit of the vine, until that day when I drink it new with you in My Father's kingdom. And when they had sung an hymn, they went out into the mount of Olives" (Matthew 26:17-20; 26-30). They sang the Hallel, Psalms 113 through 118!

The True Bread from Heaven

Because Jesus, the Messiah, is symbolized by the unleavened bread, He said: "I am the bread of life: he that cometh to Me shall never hunger; and he that believeth on Me shall never thirst" (John 6:35).

Now what are the three things that God commanded for the Passover table? They were the lamb, the unleavened bread, and bitter herbs. That is all. The most important and most significant of the three that night in Egypt was the lamb. Surely without the Passover lamb there could be no Passover, but the lamb is conspicuous at the Sedar by its absence. There has not been a lamb at the Passover feast for 1,900 years. Why? The answer is found in the Word of God: "He [the Messiah] was led as a sheep to the slaughter; and like a lamb dumb before his shearer, so opened He not His mouth" (Isaiah 53:7; Acts 8:26-40). "The next day John seeth *Jeshua* coming unto him, and saith, Behold the Lamb of God, which taketh away the sin of the world" (John 1:29). "Even Christ our passover is sacrificed for us" (1 Corinthians 5:7).

Christ was the fulfillment of the lamb slain in Egypt on that Passover night. Without the lamb then, there could have been no Passover, no deliverance. Without the Lamb of God now, there can be no true Passover and no deliverance. Without the Lamb slain, there could be no blood sprinkled and without the sprinkling of the blood, God could not have passed over; He could not have stopped the destroyer from coming into the houses of those fathers in Egypt and claiming the first-born in death. There had to be a lamb then, and there must be the Lamb now. There is no longer a lamb at the Passover feast because Jeshua Hamashiah, Jesus the Messiah, is the Lamb of God; without Him, the promised Saviour-Messiah, there can be no real Passover in this year of our Lord. A Pesach without a lamb is like an automobile without a motor, or a man without life-giving blood in his veins. That night it all depended on the shed blood of the Passover lamb. Today it all depends upon the shed blood of "Christ our passover sacrificed for us." Then, if there was no blood, there was no redemption. Now, if there is no blood, there is no redemption. What a night that was, that night in Egypt! All that happened that night was typical of God's passing over and sparing sinners, Jews and Gentiles alike, who are under the shed blood of Jeshua Hamashiah.

So the Scripture reason—God's reason—why there is no

lamb at the Passover feast is that God provided His Son as the Lamb: "Christ our passover sacrificed for us." The Passover table is both a memorial of deliverance out of Egypt and a prophecy of the coming of the Messiah. The place at the end of the table, with the empty armchair, is a constant reminder of the Coming One. How very significant!

We call upon you as individuals to believe in this Coming One, spoken of by Moses, David, and all the prophets. Believe that Christ is our true Passover and that He was sacrificed for us 1,900 years ago to deliver us from the bondage of sin and death. Know with millions of others that He arose from the dead as a guarantee of our personal redemption.

The Jewish prophetic Scriptures teach that He is coming again as the "Hope of Israel" (Acts 28:20) and "the Desire of all nations" (Haggai 2:7). In His Second Coming, He will deliver and save Israel as a nation, usher in their glorious future, and right all wrongs of the earth.

The Angel of Death Powerless

The only way those Jewish forefathers were delivered in Egypt 3,500 years ago was by believing and acting upon the message from God. They believed it was either the death of the lamb or the death of their first-born. They believed that the Lord would pass over and protect their homes from death, *if* the lamb had been slain and the blood applied. They believed God, who said, "When I see the blood, I will pass over you"! The real meaning here is, "when I see the blood, I will hover over you; I will keep the angel of death from striking your first-born."

As Jehovah protected the houses marked with the blood of the paschal lamb, so God protects those of us who believe that the shed blood of the Messiah is the only atoning blood today.

It is the same today. The message from God today is not—when I see you living a good, clean, honest life; not—when I see you living in a very religious way; not—when I see you living according to the golden rule. No, He is not saying anything like that. He is saying: "When I see the blood, I will pass over you." Either we accept God's Lamb, "Christ our passover sacrificed for us," or we receive death, the wages of sin. It is an individual matter. Whether we are Jews or Gentiles, we must believe God's message, and like those fathers in Egypt, act on it.

We therefore beseech you to look away from days and observances and behold God's Lamb, "Christ our passover sacrificed for us."

EASTER

Feast of Firstfruits

JEWISH AND GENTILE BELIEVERS the world over are celebrating Easter. We rejoice with them in the warm, gladsome, hope-giving message of which even springtime itself speaks: Life from the dead!

Easter is really the prophetic fulfillment of the third Feast of the Lord as proclaimed in Leviticus 23. There the Feast of Firstfruits, following "on the morrow after the Sabbath," points to the resurrection of the Messiah, just as Passover points to "Christ our passover sacrificed for us" (1 Corinthians 5:7). "And the Lord spake unto Moses, saying, Speak unto the children of Israel, and say unto them, When ye be come into the land which I give unto you, and shall reap the harvest thereof, then ye shall bring a *sheaf of the firstfruits* of your harvest unto the priest: And he shall wave the sheaf before the Lord, to be accepted for you: on the morrow after the sabbath the priest shall wave it" (Leviticus 23:9-11).

That is the prophecy; now note the fulfillment: "If in this life only we have hope in Christ, we are of all men most miserable. But now is Christ risen from the dead, and become the *firstfruits* of them that slept. For since by man came death, by man came also the resurrection of the dead. For as in Adam all die, even so in Christ shall all be made alive. But every man in his own order: *Christ the firstfruits;* afterward they that are Christ's at His coming" (1 Corinthians 15:19-23).

Easter (*Feast of Firstfruits*)

Notice, Israel was to bring the sheaf of the firstfruits of the harvest on the first day of the week and wave it before the Lord. Christ arose on the first day of the week. That one sheaf represented the whole harvest. The harvest is at the end of this age of sowing and planting. "Christ the firstfruits; afterward they that are Christ's at His coming," the end of the harvest.

This Feast of Firstfruits clearly points to our Lord's resurrection, and also assures all Jews and Gentiles who have put their trust in Him, "they that are Christ's at His coming," that they too will be resurrected from the dead.

Celebrated in Israel

This holy convocation, the third of the Feasts of Jehovah, had not been observed for over 2,000 years in Jewry. However, since the establishment of the State of Israel, it has been revived, most elaborately in Haifa, the nucleus of Israel's agricultural belt. This Festival of Firstfruits, as it is called in Israel, is known as *Bikkurin*. All farming communities join in the celebration, following the custom of the ancient Israelites who gave thanks for their crops. Thousands of school children present baskets of fruits and vegetables, sheaves of corn, and flowers to the Jewish National Fund, which owns much of the land of the country, holding it in trust for the people. The fund sells all offerings, using the proceeds for the never-ending task of settling new immigrants.

Passover and Easter

The word *Easter* does not occur in the Scriptures. There is a verse in the King James Version of the New Testament where the word is found, but there the word should be translated *Passover* as it is in the original text (Acts 12:4). Easter and Passover are usually close together in our calendars. Passover always falls on the fourteenth day of Nisan of the Jewish calendar. The new moon appears the first day of every month in the Jewish calendar, so on the first day of Passover, falling as it does on the fourteenth of the month, there is always a full moon. Because Easter is always on Sunday, the date varies. It always falls on the first Sunday after the first full moon following March 21, the first day of spring.

The word *Passover* in the Hebrew is *Pesach* and means *to pass or hover over.* So the teaching of Exodus 12:23 is that the Lord will protect the home where the blood of the passover lamb has been applied, thereby safeguarding that home from death.

The name *Easter* is derived from a Saxon goddess called *Eastre* and some of the Eastertide customs come from the festival of this goddess, which took place about the time we celebrate Easter. All intelligent Christians regret these pagan customs, but look beyond them and thank God for what the true Hebrew and Gentile Christian commemorates: the bodily resurrection of the Christ of God from the dead! It is this wonderful truth that causes real salvation to differ from all other religions of the world. These Jews and Gentiles who have been visited with God's salvation, as was Abraham, David, Isaiah, and all other true prophets of Israel, have a *living* Saviour. All other religious systems point to a dead founder. Salvation, therefore, should not be included in books of comparative religions, for God's salvation is incomparable!

It was Jewish individuals who first believed the truth of the resurrection of Christ. Jews were the first to be called Christians. Jewish believers were the first to proclaim this blessed message of life, hope, and immortality. This living Saviour, the Holy One of Israel, the One of whom all the prophets from Moses to Malachi spoke, said after He died and rose again, after He ascended back to Heaven: "I am He that liveth, and was dead; and, behold, I am alive for evermore, Amen" (Revelation 1:18).

Our Hope

It is because of this glorious truth that believers in Him

34

can have hope, real hope for the present and especially for the future.

Some years ago, I heard a radio address by one of New York's outstanding rabbis, really an international figure, a man whom I greatly admired. He was speaking on Easter Sunday, and referred to the hope Christians have because of the resurrection of Christ. His fine voice, usually so resonant, became very pathetic as he said, "We Jews have no hope!"

Whether you are Jew or Gentile, *you can have hope!* This hope that comes to us from the empty tomb was for the Jew *first,* and now is for both Jews and Gentiles. This hope-imparting truth is part of the gospel, the glorious gospel of God's grace; the grandest news ever proclaimed to mankind; the good tidings that God so loved us—Jews and Gentiles—that He gave His only begotten Son, Christ the Lord, who died for our sins, and was buried, and *rose again* the third day, according to the Jewish prophetic Scriptures (John 3:16; 1 Corinthians 15: 1-4).

Further Old Testament Proof

I want you to look at some of these Old Testament Scriptures and see that this most-proven fact of all history was foretold by Jewish prophets of old. In Isaiah we find this Holy One of Israel, who is there pictured as the suffering Servant of Jehovah: "He was oppressed, and He was afflicted, yet He opened not His mouth: He is brought as a lamb to the slaughter, and as a sheep before her shearers is dumb, so He openeth not His mouth. He was taken from prison and from judgment: and who shall declare His generation? For He was cut off out of the land of the living: for the transgression of my people was He stricken. And He made His grave with the wicked, and with the rich in His death; because He had done no violence, neither was any deceit in His mouth. Yet it pleased the Lord to bruise Him; He hath put Him to grief: when thou shalt make His soul an offering for sin, He shall see His seed, He shall prolong His days, and the pleasure of the Lord shall prosper in His hand. He shall see of the travail of His soul, and shall be satisfied: by His knowledge shall My righteous servant justify many, for He shall bear their iniquities" (Isaiah 53: 7-11).

In one of the Psalms, David wrote prophetically: "Therefore My heart is glad, and My glory rejoiceth: My flesh also shall rest in hope. For Thou wilt not leave My soul in hell; neither wilt Thou suffer Thine Holy One to see corruption" (Psalm 16:9-10).

The ancient patriarch Job also wrote of His resurrection: "For I know that my redeemer liveth, and that He shall stand at the latter day upon the earth: And though after my skin worms destroy this body, yet in my flesh shall I see God" (Job 19:25-26).

When we, Jews and Gentiles, believe in Him, when we believe in our hearts that Jeshua is the Jewish Messiah and the world's Saviour, and that He died for our sins and rose again according to Scriptures we have just read, then we too can say: "I know that my redeemer liveth, and that He shall stand at the latter day upon the earth: And though after my skin worms destroy my body, yet in my flesh shall I see God."

My Redeemer Lives

I know that my Redeemer lives. I know because I believe God's Word. I know He lives: one beautiful September afternoon in 1950, Mrs. Shepherd and I stood in the tomb, the very tomb, where my Saviour was buried. He was not there. He had risen as He said. You ask me how I know He lives?

> He lives, He lives, Christ Jesus lives today!
> He walks with me and talks with me
> Along life's narrow way.
> He lives, He lives, salvation to impart!
> You ask me how I know He lives?
> He lives within my heart.

It is absolutely necessary to believe in the bodily resurrection of our Saviour-Messiah. Without a heart knowledge of this glorious truth that puts salvation in a class by itself, there can be no real Passover; no forgiveness of sins; no hope; no salvation; no eternal life; no Heaven for Jews or Gentiles.

"If Christ be not raised, your faith is vain; ye are yet in your sins. Then they also which are fallen asleep in Christ are perished. If in this life only we have hope in Christ, we are of all men most miserable. But now is Christ risen from the dead, and become the *firstfruits* of them that slept. For since by man came death, by man came also the resurrection of the dead. For as in Adam all die, even so in Christ shall all be made alive. But every man in his own order: *Christ the firstfruits;* afterward they that are Christ's at His coming" (1 Corinthians 15:17-23).

Notice, both in the prophecy (Leviticus 23:10) and in the fulfillment (1 Corinthians 15:23) it is not called *firstfruit,* singular, but *firstfruits,* plural. Not one ear, but a sheaf. "Christ the firstfruits; afterward they that are Christ's at His coming." *Firstfruits* refers to the whole harvest; Christ first, afterward those of us who are true believers. So, just as Christ arose from the dead, they that are Christ's will also be resurrected from the dead at His Coming (1 Thessalonians 4:13-18; 1 Corinthians 15:23, 51-52).

It is very significant that the priest waved the sheaf before the Lord (Leviticus 23:11). The sheaf was waved "before the Lord *on the morrow after the Sabbath,"* the first day of the week, the day of Christ's resurrection. In great detail this points to happenings on that wonderful day, the most remarkable day of all history. The Gospel account pictures Mary at the empty tomb. The resurrected Messiah made Himself known to her by calling her name, "Mary!" "She turned herself, and saith unto Him, Rabboni; which is to say, Master. Jesus saith unto her, Touch me not; for I am not yet ascended to My Father" (John 20: 16-17). He had to be received by the Father before He could be appropriated by His people. The sheaf was waved before the Lord *to be accepted for you.* Not until our Lord fulfilled the type could we partake of Him as the Bread of Life.

Every lamb slain that memorable night in Egypt long ago pointed to Christ *the* Lamb of God. Every sacrificial drop of blood applied on the side posts and above the doors in Egypt, pointed to the shed blood of Christ, our Passover, sacrificed for us (1 Corinthians 5:7). But a dead Saviour can help no one. Praise God, He is not dead, for He arose from the grave. His bodily resurrection is God's receipt to us that His sacrifice was accepted and that His blood is the blood that atones for our souls (Leviticus 17:11). This glorious truth of Easter, the resurrection of Christ, is the sequel and complement to Passover, and the fulfillment of the Feast of Firstfruits!

> Up from the grave He arose,
>   With a mighty triumph o'er His foes;
> He arose a Victor from the dark domain,
>   And He lives forever with His saints to reign.
> He arose! He arose!
>   Hallelujah! Christ arose!

"If thou shalt confess with thy mouth Jesus as Lord, and shalt believe in thine heart that God hath raised Him from the dead, thou shalt be saved" (Romans 10:9).

PROCLAMATION

Establishing the State of Israel

The Jewish National Council issued the following Declaration of Independence:

"The Land of Israel was the birthplace of the Jewish people. Here their spiritual, religious, and national identity was formed. Here they achieved independence and created a culture of national and universal significance. Here they wrote and gave the Bible to the world.

"Exiled from the Land of Israel, the Jewish people remained faithful to it in all the countries of their dispersion, never ceasing to pray and hope for their return and the restoration of their national freedom.

"Impelled by this historic association, Jews strove throughout the centuries to go back to the land of their fathers and regain their statehood. In recent decades they returned in their masses. They reclaimed the wilderness, revived their language, built cities and villages, and established a vigorous and ever-growing community with its own economic and cultural life. They sought peace, yet were prepared to defend themselves. They brought the blessings of progress to all inhabitants of the country, and looked forward to sovereign independence.

"In the year 1897 the First Zionist Congress, inspired by Theodor Herzl's vision of the Jewish State, proclaimed the right of the Jewish people to national revival in their own country.

"This right was acknowledged by the Balfour Declaration

of November 2nd, 1917, and reaffirmed by the Mandate of the League of Nations, which gave explicit international recognition to the historic connection of the Jewish people with Palestine and their right to reconstitute their National Home.

"The recent holocaust, which engulfed millions of Jews in Europe, proved anew the need to solve the problem of the homelessness and lack of independence of the Jewish people by means of the re-establishment of the Jewish State, which would open the gates to all Jews and endow the Jewish people with equality of status among the family of nations.

"The survivors of the disastrous slaughter in Europe, and also Jews from other lands, have not desisted from their efforts to reach Eretz Israel in face of difficulties, obstacles, and perils; and have not ceased to urge their right to a life of dignity, freedom, and honest toil in their ancestral land.

"In the Second World War the Jewish people in Palestine made their full contribution to the struggle of the freedom-loving nations against the Nazi evil. The sacrifices of their soldiers and their war effort gained them the right to rank with the nations which founded the United Nations.

"On November 29th, 1947, the General Assembly of the United Nations adopted a Resolution requiring the establishment of a Jewish State in Palestine. The General Assembly called upon the inhabitants of the country to take all the necessary steps on their part to put the plan into effect. This recognition by the United Nations of the right of the Jewish people to establish their independent State is unassailable.

"It is the natural right of the Jewish people to lead, as do all other nations, an independent existence in its sovereign State.

"ACCORDINGLY, WE the members of the National Council, representing the Jewish people in Palestine and the World Zionist Movement, are met together in solemn assembly today, the day of the termination of the British Mandate for Palestine; and by virtue of the natural and historic right of the Jewish people and of the Resolution of the General Assembly of the United Nations,

"WE HEREBY PROCLAIM the establishment of the Jewish State in Palestine, to be called Medinath Yisrael (The State of Israel).

"WE HEREBY DECLARE that, as from the termination of the Mandate at midnight, the 14th-15th May, 1948, and pending the setting up of the duly elected bodies of the State in accordance with a Constitution to be drawn up by the Constituent Assembly not later than the 1st October, 1948, the National Council shall act as the Provisional State Council, and that the National Administration shall constitute the Provisional Government of the Jewish State, which shall be known as Israel.

"THE STATE OF ISRAEL will be open to the immigration of Jews from all countries of their dispersion; will promote the development of the country for the benefit of all its inhabitants; will be based on the principles of liberty, justice, and peace as conceived by the Prophets of Israel; will uphold the full social and political equality of all its citizens, without distinction of religion, race, or sex; will guarantee freedom of religion, conscience, education, and culture; will safeguard the Holy Places of all religions; and will loyally uphold the principles of the United Nations Charter.

"THE STATE OF ISRAEL will be ready to co-operate with the organs and representatives of the United Nations in the implementation of the Resolution of the Assembly of November 29th, 1947, and will take steps to bring about the Economic Union over the whole of Palestine.

"We appeal to the United Nations to assist the Jewish people in the building of its State, and to admit Israel into the family of nations.

"In the midst of wanton aggression, we yet call upon the Arab inhabitants of the State of Israel to preserve the ways of peace and play their part in the development of the State, on the basis of full and equal citizenship and due representation in all its bodies and institutions, provisional and permanent.

"We extend our hand in peace and neighborliness to all the neighboring states and their peoples, and invite them to co-operate with the independent Jewish nation for the common good of all. The State of Israel is prepared to make its contribution to the progress of the Middle East as a whole.

"Our call goes out to the Jewish people all over the world to rally to our side in the task of immigration and development, and to stand by us in the great struggle for the fulfilment of the dream of generations for the redemption of Israel.

"With trust in Almighty God, we set our hand to this Declaration, at this Session of the Provisional State Council, on the soil of the Homeland, in the city of Tel-Aviv, on this Sabbath Eve, the fifth of Iyar, 5708, the fourteenth day of May, 1948."

INDEPENDENCE DAY

Israel's Regathering

THE MIRACLE OF THE TWENTIETH CENTURY is what has happened in the Middle East during the past five decades. The Jewish people who were divinely expelled from the land of their fathers 2,000 years ago, are being regathered according to the prophetic Word. It cannot now be said of the great majority of Jewish people:

> Scattered by God's avenging hand,
> Afflicted and forlorn,
> Sad wanderers from their pleasant land,
> Do Judah's children mourn.

Independence Day is the time when the nations of the world salute the State of Israel. It is also a Memorial Day in Israel. The day is set apart to remember the soldiers who died in the War of Liberation and who are buried on Mount Herzl and elsewhere throughout the state. The ministry of defense sends personal messages of condolence to all families who lost men and women in the country's struggle to maintain freedom. On the eve of the holiday, thousands make the pilgrimage and stand before Herzl's grave on a high plateau, beautiful for situation and overlooking the city of Jerusalem. At night, celebrations are launched by the kindling of "Independence Torches," a ceremony in which various immigrant groups fittingly take part, as a symbol of Israel's main purpose and achievement.

The establishment of the State of Israel began on November 29, 1947, when the United Nations Organization voted to partition the land of Palestine, as it was then called. Was that according to prophecy? Read Joel 3:2! The partitioning plan was to become effective one year from that date. However, the British Mandate came to an end and Palestine was left without law and order. The police and fire departments and postal system disintegrated and everyone could do that which was right in his own eyes. Conditions were explosive, but Jewish people have a faculty of meeting every emergency. Their leaders called key men throughout the land to gather in Tel Aviv. They went into an historic session that lasted all afternoon and far into the night. The outcome—Israel's Declaration of Independence. According to the Jewish calendar that was Iyar 5, 5708 (May 14, 1948).

The new Nation of Israel was immediately recognized by world powers and on May 11, 1949, was received as a member nation of the United Nations Organization. Since then they have celebrated their elaborate tenth anniversary of statehood and their "Bar Mitzvah."

Israel's Bar Mitzvah

Just as a *Bar Mitzvah* speaks for himself, Israel spoke, as it were, and delivered an impressive *"Bar Mitzvah* address." It was a comprehensive account of the steady advance on the road to self-sufficiency and progress.

To the embarrassment of the United Nations, the seat of government was moved from Tel Aviv to Jerusalem. A clause in the Petitioning Plan specifically stated that the entire city of Jerusalem was to be an international city ruled by the United Nations Organization. That was a remarkable fulfillment of the Lord's words in Luke 21:24: "Jerusalem shall be trodden down of the Gentiles, until the times of the Gentiles be fulfilled." This statement rules out any possibility of truth in the British-Israel theory!

Is This According to Prophecy?

The student of divine prophecy was not surprised by these

momentous happenings in the Middle East. At the turn of the century, Dr. William L. Pettingill wrote a book entitled, *Israel, Jehovah's Covenant People.* One would think this book was written since Israel established herself as a nation. Dr. Pettingill simply quoted those prophecies regarding the regathering of the Jewish people and their restoration to the land.

The clearest prophecy regarding the regathering is to be found in Ezekiel 36 and 37. Remember, this prophecy was written about 2,500 years ago. God said through the prophet: "I scattered them among the heathen [Gentile nations], and they were dispersed through the countries" (Ezekiel 36:19).

The final dispersion took place in A.D. 70 when the Roman general Titus savagely conquered Jerusalem, destroyed the Temple, and scattered the people of Israel. They became the people of the wandering feet.

That prophecy also reveals both the heart and faithfulness of God: "But I had pity for Mine holy name, which the house of Israel had profaned among the heathen [Gentiles], whither they went. Therefore say unto the house of Israel, Thus saith the Lord God; I do not this for your sakes . . . but for Mine holy name's sake. . . . For I will take you from among the heathen [Gentiles], and gather you out of all countries, and will bring you into your own land" (Ezekiel 36:21-24).

The establishment of the State of Israel is not the fulfillment of these prophecies. It is a political or Zionist movement; but it is certainly the beginning of the great exodus described in Jeremiah 23:7-8: "Therefore, behold, the days come, saith the Lord, that they shall no more say, The Lord liveth, which brought up the children of Israel out of the land of Egypt; But, The Lord liveth, which brought up and which led the seed of the house of Israel out of the north country, and from all countries whither I had driven them; and they shall dwell in their own land."

While the establishment of the State of Israel is not actually the fulfillment of this remarkable prophecy, it is most significant and important. It is absolutely necessary that Israel be established as a nation before the Lord Jesus can come for His own, as described in 1 Thessalonians 4:14-18. According to 2 Thessalonians 2, the "man of sin," the "son of perdition," will be revealed after the Church is raptured. This "wicked one," "the prince," will make a covenant with the Jewish people. He will break the covenant in the middle of the "seven weeks of years," and then will be ushered in the terrible "time of Jacob's trouble," spoken of by Jeremiah the prophet (30:7; Daniel 9:24-27). To whom could this Antichrist have gone to make an official covenant before the establishment of the State of Israel?

The Jewish people were divided politically, for there are Zionists and non-Zionists. They were divided religiously, for there are Orthodox, Conservative, Reform, and others. And furthermore, they were scattered all over the world. Today this beast emperor, "the prince," could land a jet airliner from anywhere and in a few hours appear before the Knesset, the Israeli Parliament in Jerusalem, and make an official covenant with the nation. The Jewish people in the land today are prepared to receive this Antichrist. All of this causes us to know how very late it is according to God's prophetic timetable!

God is getting the Jews back to the land, not because they are turning to Him, or because they deserve it, but because of His Holy Name. It is not because of their faithfulness, but because of His faithfulness. God always deals with His creatures on this basis. We deserve nothing from Him but judgment. He deals with us according to His mercy and not according to our merit. His Word cannot be broken.

The Lord God will move Heaven and earth to cause His Word to be fulfilled. He allowed World War I to prepare the land for His people. That war opened the door for Jewish people to go to the land of their fathers. World War II prepared the people for the land, for the great majority of Jewish people, especially those living in Europe, had no desire to go to the land. And there will be another World War that will prepare the Jewish people in the land for their Messiah. Many prophetic students and military men believe World War III will end in the battle of Armageddon, which would mean that World War III would be the last world war. All this proves that God is interested in the nations of the world primarily as they affect and touch His covenant people, Israel.

The latter part of Ezekiel 36 gives the ultimate of God's plan and purpose for Israel as a nation. It is a prophecy of a future day when God will give them a new heart and put His Spirit within them. Then follows the thirty-seventh chapter that gives details of their regathering and national salvation. We also have here the prophecy of the two sticks coming together, representing Judah, the two tribes; and Israel, the ten tribes.

The first part of Ezekiel 37 is being fulfilled. Two million from over eighty countries have gone back to the land. We believe the "sticks" are coming together: i.e., there are representatives of the twelve tribes in the land today. They are there in the exact spiritual condition as foretold in this prophecy. They are there in unbelief. There is no breath (Spirit) in them.

Happy Hatikvah

Ezekiel 37:11 reveals a heart cry of the Jewish people: "Our bones are dried, and our hope is lost: we are cut off for our parts."

How wonderful that we have lived to see the hope of Israel's national anthem being fulfilled. *Hatikvah* means *the hope*. That stirring anthem contains nine stanzas which speak the longing for Zion and the desire to return to it. The refrain is:

> Yet is our hope not lost,
> The ancient hope,
> To dwell in the land of our fathers,
> In the city where David encamped.

Israel's true hope is not the hope to dwell in the land, but is all part of God's plan for His covenant people. The Messiah is their true hope, but with Job they are saying, "where is now

47

my hope" (Job 17:15). Israel's heart will continue to be sick (Proverbs 13:12) until they say with David of old, "Lord, what wait I for? my hope is in Thee" (Psalm 39:7).

An Eternal Salute

The whole world is amazed over Israel's accomplishments on that little strip of barren land, surrounded by enemies determined to wipe them off the map of the turbulent Middle East. Phenomenal progress has been achieved, not only by inspiration, but by perspiration; by blood and tears! Out of political and diplomatic courtesy, nations year after year salute the State of Israel.

As wonderful as their political birth was, their spiritual birth will far surpass it. At their spiritual birth, all Gentile nations will see Israel's righteousness, and all rulers will behold her glory (Isaiah 62:2). Then, "ten men shall take hold out of all languages of the nations, even shall take hold of the skirt of him that is a Jew, saying, We will go with you: for we have heard that God is with you" (Zechariah 8:23).

How different that will be compared to the attitude of ten Gentile men today toward one Jew. Today they persecute, condemn, and discriminate against them; but in that future day men will behold the Jewish people living godly, righteous lives; they will see Israel enjoying the glory of their redemption and being a blessing to all the families of the earth. Then ten men will beg one such Jew to allow them to go with him, for all will know that God is with the redeemed nation of Israel. Think of it, ten *goyim* and one *yehuda!*

No matter how elaborate the festivities of Israel's anniversary, they cannot be compared with the glory of that future day of the nation's spiritual rebirth. But in that future day of Israel's salvation, how different it will be. The Lord God tells us about conditions in that future day: "Many nations shall come, and say, Come, and let us go up to the mountain [i.e., the kingdom] of the Lord, and to the house of the God of Jacob; and He will teach us of His ways, and we will walk in His paths: for the law shall go forth of Zion, and the word of the Lord from Jerusalem. And He shall judge among many people, and rebuke strong nations afar off; and they shall beat their swords into plowshares, and their spears into pruninghooks: nation shall not lift up a sword against nation, neither shall they learn war any more. But they shall sit every man under his vine and under his fig tree; and none shall make them afraid: for the mouth of the Lord of hosts hath spoken it. For all peoples do now walk in the name of their god, but then shall walk in the name of Jehovah our Elohim forever (Micah 4:2-5).

What a contrast to conditions in Israel today is this picture of peace and safety in that future day of Israel's spiritual rebirth. There will be peace and safety *then* because righteousness will reign. And note what the prophetic Word has to say about the land: "And the desolate land shall be tilled, whereas it lay desolate in the sight of all that passed by. And they shall say, This land that was desolate is become like the garden of Eden; and the waste and desolate and ruined cities are become fenced, and are inhabited" (Ezekiel 36:34-35 .

When and How of Israel's Spiritual Rebirth

Now consider just two more things: First, *when* will Israel's spiritual rebirth take place? Secondly, *how* will it take place?

Israel's political rebirth took place on May 14, 1948. When will her spiritual rebirth occur, or when will this prophecy of peace and safety, prosperity, and righteousness be enjoyed in Israel?

That wonderful day will dawn after the time of Jacob's trouble, as spoken by Jeremiah the prophet (30:7). At the end of that tribulation, which will be shortened for the sake of the believing Jewish people of that day (Matthew 24:22), the Lord Messiah will come as the Son of Man. He comes at that time as King of kings and Lord of lords to set up His righteous kingdom described by Isaiah in chapters 11 and 12; Jeremiah in chapter 23; Zechariah; and other Jewish prophets. We believe the time of His Coming is very close at hand. The prophetic clock tells us it is one minute to twelve!

How will Israel's spiritual rebirth be accomplished? We know how her political rebirth came about in 1948; but how will her spiritual rebirth be effected and how will there be safety and security in Israel?

The answer can be found in many of the Old Testament prophecies. Many places in Jewish Scriptures we find all the answers to our question of how Israel's spiritual rebirth will be accomplished. We will look at just one of these Scriptures: Zechariah 12. In that chapter we find the phrase, "in that day," used several times. It refers to the day of the Second Coming to earth of Israel's Messiah, Jehovah-Tsidkenu, the Lord our Righteousness (Jeremiah 23:6). "In that day" great armies will be in a crushing siege against Israel, and the nation's destruction seems inevitable. And it shall come to pass "in that day" that the Lord Messiah will come, and with the breath of His mouth will destroy all the nations that will be lined up against Israel. The remnant of Jewish people, comprising the nation of Israel "in that day," will recognize their Messiah (Zechariah 13:8-9). They will know Him by His nail prints; they will see *then* that He is indeed the One who was pierced on God's altar of sacrifice. They will look to Him and be regenerated—born again. Read through the prophecy in Zechariah 12 and 13 and see that that future day of Israel's salvation is the ultimate Yom Kippur, the final Day of Atonement. There will be more intense mourning and bitterness and sorrowing for sin than in any previous Day of Atonement. This remarkable Jewish prophecy in Zechariah goes on to say: "In that day there shall be a fountain opened to the house of David and to the inhabitants of Jerusalem for sin and uncleanness" (Zechariah 13:1).

The finished work of Israel's Messiah on Calvary 1,900 years ago will then avail for the remnant, the nation of Israel.

That fountain is the atoning blood of Christ, and will be effectively and effectually opened for Israel. It is His shed blood that will cleanse Israel from all sin. It is that blood that alone atones for the soul (Leviticus 17:11).

God has only one way of salvation, whether it be in that future day for Israel as a nation, or for individual Jews and Gentiles today. That one way of salvation is—Jeshua Hamashiah. Obey Him, who said through the prophet Isaiah: "Look unto Me, and be ye saved, all the ends of the earth: for I am God, and there is none else" (Isaiah 45:22).

That is the way the nation of Israel will be saved in that future day and that is the only way any Jew or Gentile can be saved today. "Behold the Lamb of God, which taketh away the sin of the world" (John 1:29).

It is our heart's desire and prayer that Jewish people will not only observe the anniversary of the establishment of the State of Israel, but that they will consider their individual salvation. Each individual, Jew and Gentile, must look to the Lamb of God *now* to be visited with God's great salvation. He—Jeshua, the Messiah—bore our sins in His own body on the tree (1 Peter 2:24). Believe in Him and you will have an eternal celebration in your heart and life.

SHABUOTH

Feast of Pentecost

SHABUOTH IS A GAY HOLIDAY in Jewry. It falls on Sivan*
6 and 7 in the Jewish calendar. This festive day is also called
Feast of Weeks (Exodus 34:22) as Shabuoth means *weeks*.
It is also known as the Feast of Pentecost, because it falls fifty
days after Firstfruits, and the word Pentecost means *fifty* or
fifty days.

In Bible times, the firstfruits of the fields and orchards
from the spring harvest were brought to the Temple as an
offering to the Lord. It is celebrated today in synagogues and
Jewish homes as a thanksgiving festival. Because the beautiful
story of Ruth is laid in the time of the barley harvest, the book
of Ruth is read in synagogues on the second day.

During the Temple worship, the children of Israel brought
a sheaf of the firstfruits of the spring harvest and offered it
to the Lord. It was considered a day of Israel's dedication. No
doubt, that is why confirmation ceremonies for Jewish young
people are held on Shabuoth.

The Law Given

Traditionally, the holiday is also the commemoration of
the giving of the Ten Commandments. It is the *zeman mattan
torathena,* the *time of the giving of the law*. That is why the

---

*The Jewish month, Sivan, corresponds with May and sometimes
takes in the early part of June.

eve of the first day, Sivan 6, is observed by many Jewish people with the reading of the Scriptures. In some synagogues the entire night is spent in such study. In all synagogues the Ten Commandments are publicly read at the morning service. Just before the reading of the Ten Commandments, a verse from an eleventh-century poem is sung. Many of you will recognize the words of this fine old hymn, "Love of God":

> Could we with ink the ocean fill,
> Were every blade of grass a quill,
> Were the whole world of parchment made,
> And every man a scribe by trade,
> To write the love of God above
> Would drain the ocean dry;
> Nor could the scroll contain the whole,
> Though stretched from sky to sky.

How true, God's love stretches from Heaven to earth; it is deeper than the deepest sea. Any scroll telling of the love of God, if it could contain the whole, would stretch from planet to planet and from pole to pole.

The Feast in Prophecy

The Biblical basis for this happy holiday is found in Leviticus, chapter 23, where the seven Feasts of Jehovah are given: "And ye shall count unto you from the morrow after the sabbath, from the day that ye brought the sheaf of the wave-offering; seven sabbaths shall be complete: Even unto the morrow after the seventh sabbath shall ye number fifty days; and ye shall offer a new meal-offering unto the Lord. Ye shall bring out of your habitations two wave-loaves of two tenth deals: they shall be of fine flour; they shall be baken with leaven; they are the firstfruits unto the Lord. . . . And ye shall proclaim on the selfsame day, that it may be an holy convocation unto you: ye shall do no servile work therein: it shall be a statute for ever in all your dwellings throughout your generations. And when ye reap the harvest of your land, thou shalt not make clean riddance of the corners of thy field when thou reapest, neither shalt thou gather any gleaning of thy harvest:

thou shalt leave them unto the poor, and to the stranger: I am the Lord your God" (Leviticus 23:15-17, 21-22).

Just as Passover and Unleavened Bread have prophetic significance, and look to "Christ our passover sacrificed for us" (1 Corinthians 5:7); and Firstfruits points to His resurrection; this Feast of Jehovah, Shabuoth, directs us to the Day of Pentecost that fell exactly fifty days after His resurrection. The Day of Pentecost was the birthday of the Church when the Holy Spirit, the Ruach K'doshen, came to unite the Jewish believers of that day into one loaf or body. The scriptural account of the fulfillment of Shabuoth is found in the beginning of the book of Acts, which is the divine history of the early Church.

The Feast in Fulfillment

"And when the day of *Pentecost* was fully come, they were all with one accord in one place. And suddenly there came a sound from heaven as of a rushing mighty wind, and it filled all the house where they were sitting. And there appeared unto them cloven tongues like as of fire, and it sat upon each of them. And they were all filled with the Holy Spirit, and began to speak with other tongues, as the Spirit gave them utterance. And there were dwelling at Jerusalem Jews, devout men, out of every nation under heaven. Now when this was noised abroad, the multitude came together, and were confounded, because that every man heard them speak in his own language. And they were all amazed and marvelled, saying one to another, Behold, are not all these which speak Galileans? . . . We do hear them speak in our tongues the wonderful works of God. And they were all amazed, and were in doubt, saying one to another, What meaneth this? Others mocking said, These men are full of new wine" (Acts 2:1-13).

The great Jewish Pentecostal preacher, the Apostle Peter, stood up and answered the question, "What meaneth this?" Study the record and see how he read from the Old Testament and proved conclusively that this phenomenon was the beginning of a mighty work of the Holy Spirit in the Church, and that their Messiah is the Head of that body: "As the body is one, and hath many members, and all the members of that one body, being many, are one body: so also is Christ. For by one Spirit are we all baptized into one body, whether we be Jews or Gentiles" (1 Corinthians 12:12-13).

Shabuoth points to Christ as the Head of the Church that came into existence on the Day of Pentecost. The Holy Spirit united the believers in that body and, since then, all true Jewish and Gentile believers are not only indwelt by the Holy Spirit, but are baptized into that same body.

In the Passover preparations, all leaven had to be removed from Jewish homes. The second Feast of Jehovah, Unleavened Bread, is combined with the Passover observances. There could be no leaven there, for leaven is a type of sin. In Christ, our Passover, there is no sin, for He is the Holy One of Israel, the spotless Lamb of God. But in this Feast of Pentecost, they were specifically instructed to bake the wave-loaves with leaven. There is no sin in the Head of the Church; but who can deny that there is sin in the members. And there will be sin in the members of His body until we will be made like Him (Philippians 3:20-21; 1 John 3:2). That is why the Apostle Paul exhorted the Church at Corinth: "Your glorying is not good. Know ye not that a little leaven leaveneth the whole lump? Purge out therefore the old leaven, that ye may be a new lump, as ye are unleavened. For even Christ our passover is sacrificed for us" (1 Corinthians 5:6-7).

Keep the Feast

Believing Jews and Gentiles, those who have been born into the family of God through faith in the crucified and risen Saviour, those who have been baptized into the body of Christ, should keep this Feast of Pentecost by: "Endeavouring to keep the unity of the Spirit in the bond of peace. . . . And grieve not the holy Spirit of God, whereby ye are sealed unto the day of redemption. Let all bitterness, and wrath, and anger, and clamour, and evil speaking, be put away from you, with all malice: And be ye kind one to another, tenderhearted, forgiving one another, even as God for Christ's sake hath forgiven you" (Ephesians 4:3, 30-32).

Our message to Jewish friends who have not believed in the Lord Jeshua as their Saviour-Messiah, is to look beyond the synagogue observances and see the One to whom Shabuoth points. These are but shadows. The substance has come, so look to Him. "Let no man therefore judge you in meat, or in drink, or in respect of an holyday, or of the new moon, or of the sabbath: Which are a shadow of things to come: but the body is Christ" (Colossians 2:16-17).

And our heart's desire and prayer for Gentiles is that they, too, will keep the feast: believe on the Lord Jesus Christ who appeared 1,900 years ago to put away sin by the sacrifice of Himself (Hebrews 9:26). They, too, by God's infinite grace and mercy can be members of that wonderful body of which He is the Head, and know that they are bound for Heaven (John 14:6). "Keep the feast . . . with the unleavened bread of sincerity and truth."

Eat the scroll, as did Ezekiel. "Then did I eat it," said the prophet, "and it was in my mouth as honey for sweetness" (Ezekiel 3:1-3). The entrance of God's Word gives light (Psalm 119:130), and enables Jew and Gentile to behold the Substance, the One whom this holiday foreshadows, even Christ the Lord. "O taste and see that the Lord is good: blessed is the man that trusteth in him" (Psalm 34:8).

ROSH HASHANAH—NEW YEAR

Feast of Blowing of Trumpets

THIS HOLIDAY falls on the first day of Tishri, the seventh month in the Jewish calendar. It is in the fall of the year and corresponds for the most part with our September.

Rosh Hashanah brings happy memories to us. A few years ago we were in Jerusalem and saw hundreds of Jewish people —men, women, and children—coming from different sections of that new, fast-growing modern city toward the railroad station and then trekking along that narrow road down into the valley of Hinnom and up to Mount Zion. They came from all parts of Israel to pray at the tomb of David on Mount Zion. This hallowed spot in Israel was the place where they wailed and prostrated themselves as they prayed. The Wailing Wall (Western Wall) was then in the Hashemite Kingdom of Jordan, and no Jewish people were permitted in that Arab country. We heard the tramp of feet from early morning until evening, and watched pious Jews with their *peyoth* (side curls), some dressed in plus-fours and *kapole* (long black alpaca coats) and *streimel* (large round fur hats). This procession continued for two days, for this is a two-day holiday in Jewry. At the close of the second day, we visited the largest synagogue in Jerusalem. One of the assistant rabbis very graciously greeted us. He showed Mrs. Shepherd the way to the balcony where the women sit, and after placing a *yamulka* (black scull cap) on my head and draping my shoulders with a *tallith* (prayer shawl), led me to a seat

57

near the front, and explained parts of the ceremonies to me. It was all most interesting and we shall ever thank our Lord that He made it possible for us to visit that miracle land. We will always be grateful, too, for the gracious way the Jewish people in the land received us.

There are many more people in Jerusalem going through these ceremonies this year, for the population has greatly increased during the years since we were there; also, many more American Jews will visit Israel during this holiday season.

All over the world, wherever it is possible, Jewish people will go to their synagogue, recite long prayers, confess their sins of omission and sins of commission (*ne al chet*), and pray God, "that He should inscribe them for the coming year."

Our best wishes are extended to them and it is our prayer that in the providence of God, they will have a blessed year. God grant that all of our Jewish friends will have less tears and fears than in past tragic years. So to our Jewish friends, we say, "Rosh Hashanah, Good Sabbath to you!" No one can predict what will happen in the Middle East in the immediate future and how it will effect Israel, but we do know what the future holds for Israel because we know the God who holds the future for His covenant people. So again, we pray the God of Abraham, Isaac, and Jacob that He should inscribe them for the coming year, the traditional Jewish greeting (*L'Shanah Tovah Tikoseivu*).

A Far Cry from Biblical Judaism

The way in which Jewry celebrates this holy convocation described in Leviticus 23, for the first day of the seventh month, is one of many sad evidences that the Jewish people have drifted far from Biblical Judaism. As we observe this, we realize that Christians live in glass houses and dare not throw stones at our Lord's brethren after the flesh. Christianity as observed today is also a far cry from New Testament Christianity. That is why we never try to convert Jews or Gentiles to Christianity: we point them to Christ that they might be visited with true salvation.

The Biblical New Year for Israel is the first day of the first month, called Nisan in the Jewish calendar (called Nisan in Esther 3:7, and Abib in Exodus 13:4 and 34:18). "And the Lord spake unto Moses and Aaron in the land of Egypt, saying, This month shall be unto you the beginning of months: it shall be the first month of the year to you" (Exodus 12:1-2).

How very clear this is. Today the Jewish people call the first day of the seventh month (Tishri), Rosh Hashanah (Rosh means *head* or *beginning*). The Jewish people do not refer to Nisan 1 as a New Year's Day, but there really are two New Year's Days in Jewry: the Biblical one, Nisan 1, and the Civil one, Tishri 1. However, only the latter, occurring in the fall of the year, is recognized today as New Year.

It is generally believed that a change, from Nisan 1 to Tishri 1, was made during the tenth or eleventh century. The rabbis of that day believed the Lord God created the world in the month of Tishri. It would seem that is why the people who returned to the land with Nehemiah were gathered together on the "first day of the seventh month," Tishri (Nehemiah 8:2). They met to hear the book of the law read. The classic verse on homiletics is found in this account: "So they read in the book in the law of God distinctly, and gave the sense, and caused them to understanding the reading" (Nehemiah 8:8).

The Blowing of Trumpets

An explanation of trumpet blowing is found in Numbers 10. The trumpets were blown in Israel for the calling of the assembly; to sound an alarm; to prepare the people for battle; and as was done at the Feast of Trumpets, as a memorial before their God. The instructions for observing this fifth Feast of Jehovah are found in Leviticus 23: "Speak unto the children of Israel, saying, In the seventh month, in the first day of the month, shall ye have a sabbath, a memorial of blowing of trumpets, an holy convocation. Ye shall do no servile work therein: but ye shall offer an offering made by fire unto the Lord" (Leviticus 23:24-25).

This blowing of trumpets was a memorial of God's grace to Abraham when He substituted a ram to be sacrificed instead of his son, Isaac (Genesis 22). Therefore the Jewish people today blow a ram's horn on Rosh Hashanah.

This feast was not only to be observed as a memorial, but like all the seven Feasts of Jehovah, it is a prophecy. It points to the present regathering of Israel. From Numbers 10:1-10 we learn that the blowing of the trumpet was for the calling and gathering of the people (Isaiah 43:5-6; Ezekiel 36: 24). Almost two million have been gathered from over eighty countries and are now in the land of Israel. It almost seems that we should hear God's trumpet blasts!

The blowing of trumpets also points to the return of the Messiah; so, like all these Feasts of Jehovah, this one points to Him, Christ the Lord. The present regathering and the establishment of the State of Israel are strong evidences that His Coming is close at hand.

At His coming in the air for His redeemed ones, the "trumpet of God" will sound forth (1 Thessalonians 4:16; 1 Corinthians 15:51-52). We are not looking for signs any longer; we are listening for the trumpet call and the shout!

A Significant Long Space

It should be noted that there is a long space of time between the Feast of Pentecost and the one we are considering, the Blowing of Trumpets. The time that elapsed between the two Feasts is from the spring to the fall. Could that be symbolic of the long period from the formation of the Church on the day of Pentecost to the present regathering of Israel and the soon trumpet blast calling Christ's own blood-bought ones to "Rise Up, My love, My fair one, and come away" (Song of Solomon 2:10)?

Rosh Hashanah (New Year's Day)

Before the Lord Messiah went back to the Father after dying for our sins, and being raised again, He made two promises to His disciples. One, the promise of the Holy Spirit, that was fulfilled on the Day of Pentecost. The other was, "I will come again" (John 14:3). There has been a space of almost 2,000 years between the fulfillment of these two promises. Just as the one was literally fulfilled, we can rest assured the other will be. In fact, it has started with the present regathering of Israel. This makes this word of prophecy more sure (2 Peter 1:19 R.V.). Every truly born-again Jew and Gentile responds with the beloved apostle of old, "Even so, come, Lord Jesus" (Revelation 22:20).

The Feast of Trumpets has started to be fulfilled in the regathering of Israel back to the land of promise, and it will be completely fulfilled in the Second Coming of the Lord Jesus Christ.

Trumpets Giving Uncertain Sounds

God's trumpets can always be depended upon. However, there are voices and sounds of trumpets abroad today that are uncertain and even false. We need to beware: "For if the trumpet give an uncertain sound, who shall prepare himself to the battle? (1 Corinthians 14:8).

Who can deny that we are in a battle? But it is good to know "the battle is the Lord's" (1 Samuel 17:47).

The alarm to be sounded in these last days is: "Prepare to meet thy God, O Israel" (Amos 4:12). "Blow the trumpet in Zion" (Joel 2:15).

Whether you are a Jew or a Gentile, heed the call as we sound the alarm, as we blow the trumpet. Recognize that you are a lost sinner and that you cannot save yourself, either by observances of holy days, good deeds, or alms giving. Then hear the good news that these Feasts of Jehovah declare. Christ is your Passover who was sacrificed for you (1 Corinthians 5:7); He arose from the dead, and sent the Holy Spirit to convict you of sin: of sin, because you believe not on Him (John 16:7-9). "He came unto His own, and His own received Him not. But as many as received Him, to them gave He power to become the sons of God, even to them that believe on His name: Which were born, not of blood, nor of the will of the flesh, nor of the will of man, but of God" (John 1:11-13).

Obey this Scripture and you will enjoy a new day, a new year, an eternal New Year, where there are joys and pleasures forevermore (Psalm 16:11).

See pages 65-66, *Modern Day Observance*.

YOM KIPPUR

Day of Atonement

TISHRI is the month* of important and solemn holidays among Jewish people. There is Rosh Hashanah, the Jewish New Year, and now we come to the most solemn of all holy days, Yom Kippur, the Day of Atonement, Tishri 10. And on the fourteenth day of this month Tishri, there is Succoth.

The Day of Atonement is really the only scriptural fast day. This day is glorious in its antiquity. It speeds our minds back over the centuries to the days of Moses. According to the divine commandment, this tenth day of Tishri, the Day of Atonement, should be celebrated quite differently from the way it is kept today. Let me give you these instructions as God spoke to Moses 3,500 years ago, and recorded for us in Leviticus, chapter 23. Here we have the correct and only divinely authorized mode of observance of this holy ceremony:

Biblical Observance

"And the Lord spake unto Moses, saying, Also on the tenth day of this seventh month there shall be a day of atonement: it shall be an holy convocation unto you; and ye shall afflict your souls, and offer an offering made by fire unto the Lord. And ye shall do no work in that same day: for it is a day of atonement, to make an atonement for you before the Lord your God. For whatever soul it be that shall not be afflicted in that same day, he shall be cut off from among his people. . . .

*September and sometimes early in October.

Ye shall do no manner of work; it shall be a statute for ever throughout your generations in all your dwellings. It shall be unto you a sabbath of rest, and ye shall afflict your souls: in the ninth day of the month at even, from even unto even, shall ye celebrate your sabbath" (Leviticus 23:26-32).

And now in chapter 16 of Leviticus we find it specifically stated just what was to be done on the Day of Atonement. This was the great solemn day when the high priest went into the holy of holies in the Temple. He sacrificed a bullock and the second goat, then sprinkled the most holy place, the veil, the altar, and cleansed them from all defilement. The lots had been cast upon the two goats. The one upon which the lot fell was sacrificed unto the Lord as a sin offering; and the other one the priest was to present before the Lord, laying his hands upon its head and confessing over it the sins of the congregation so that it would bear away, unto a land not inhabited, all the sins of the people. That one was called the scapegoat. And this was done in order to *make atonement* (Kaphar), from which developed the name *Yom Kippur*.

Clearly the only basis of true atonement was, and is, blood. "The life of the flesh is in the blood; and I have given it to you upon the altar to make an atonement for your souls: for it is the blood that maketh an atonement for the soul" (Leviticus 17:11).

The Talmud is in full agreement: "There is no atonement but by blood," we read in "Yoma" (chapter 5-a). There can be no Yom Kippur, Day of Atonement, without Yom Kippur, blood of atonement.

Are these instructions carried out today by the Jewish people? No! Why not? If you asked me that question, I would answer, "They do not take the two goats, kill one and send the scapegoat off, after the sins of Israel were typically laid on him, for the same reason they do not kill the Passover lamb at Passover time." They do neither because *the* sacrifice, the One toward whom these sacrifices and ceremonies pointed, has come and literally fulfilled the types. In the language of Scripture, these ceremonies *were a shadow of things to come* (Colossians 2:17); really of some One to come. As coming events cast their shadows before, the Messiah of Israel cast His shadow all through the Old Testament. Now that He has come, we look to the Substance and not to the shadow.

Impossible to Observe Today

For nineteen hundred years it has been impossible to carry out the Biblical instructions for the Day of Atonement because there has been no Temple. In A.D. 70, the Temple was destroyed, and the prophecy uttered by Hosea has been in effect these twenty centuries. "For the children of Israel shall abide many days without a king, and without a prince, and without a sacrifice, and without an image, and without an ephod, and without teraphim: Afterwards shall the children of Israel return, and seek the Lord their God, and David their King; and shall fear the Lord and His goodness in the latter days" (Hosea 3:4-5).

What a remarkable prophecy; and to think that we have lived to see this "afterward" at least start to be fulfilled!

The ten days between Rosh Hashanah and Yom Kippur are known as "the Awesome Days." They are the ten days of repentance when the Jewish people were commanded to search their hearts and afflict their souls. In Biblical times the emphasis on this was so strong, that anyone who did not afflict his soul would suffer death. Hear again the pronouncement: "For whatsoever soul it be that shall not be afflicted in that same day, he shall be cut off from among his people" (Leviticus 23:29).

Where is there real affliction of soul today? The very fact that Jewish people do not so afflict their souls and are not "cut off," proves that God is dealing with both Jews and Gentiles under a new covenant.

Modern Day Observance

On Tishri 1, or Rosh Hashanah, the custom today

is for the Jewish people to make atonements of their own. They gather at watering places to perform the symbolic ritual of casting away their sins (Micah 7:19). This is known as *Tashlikh*. A man takes a rooster and a woman a hen. Each one swings the fowl around his or her head, saying, "This is my substitute; this is my commutation; this rooster, or hen, goeth to death; but may I be gathered and enter into a long and happy life and into peace." This is called *Kapparah,* which means atoning sacrifice. All this is done as a sign of confession of their sin. The other substitutes for atoning sacrifice in modern Jewry are: repentance, prayer, charity, do justly. The most solemn prayer of all Jewish ritual is said on Yom Kippur. It is known as *Kol Nidre,* meaning *all vows.* The cantor intones: "All vows, bonds, oaths, devotions, promises, penalites, and obligations: wherewith we have vowed, sworn, devoted, and bound ourselves: from this Day of Atonement unto the next Day of Atonement, may it come unto us for good: lo, all these, we repent us in them. They shall be absolved, released, annulled, made void, and of none effect: They shall not be binding nor shall they have any power. Our vows shall not be vows: and our oaths shall not be oaths."

We are deeply moved with compassion by these confessions and obligations. Would to God I could get all to see that the Lord God can forgive sin only through the shedding of blood, and not through a day, or anything we do or could do. He said, "When I see the *blood,* I will pass over you" (Exodus 12:13). "It is the *blood* that maketh an atonement [covering] for the soul" (Leviticus 17:11). "Without shedding of *blood* there is no remission" (Hebrews 9:22). In fulfillment of all the Jewish prophecies concerning real atoning sacrifice, God sent His Son 1,900 years ago to provide the only acceptable sacrifice. "He was wounded for our transgressions, He was bruised for our iniquities: the chastisement of our peace was upon Him; and with His stripes we are healed. All we like sheep have gone astray; we have turned every one to his own way;

and the Lord hath laid on Him the iniquity of us all. He was oppressed, and he was afflicted, yet He opened not His mouth: He is brought as a lamb to the slaughter, and as a sheep before her shearers is dumb, so He opened not His mouth" (Isaiah 53:5-7).

Not only does all Scripture evidence the truth that Jeshua is the promised Messiah, spoken of here by Isaiah, but all facts of history, and the experience of millions, point to this most important and established truth of all time. Jeshua the Christ came just at the time Moses said He would come (Genesis 49: 10). He could come only before the scepter departed from Judah. It did depart religiously in A.D. 70 when the Temple was destroyed. He came of the tribe of Judah (Genesis 49:10; Hebrews 7:14). He came by the very means Isaiah boldly proclaimed, the virgin's womb (Isaiah 7:14; Matthew 1:18-25). He was born in the city foretold by Micah, Bethlehem (Micah 5:2; Matthew 2:1). He was "cut off" at the very time Daniel foretold (Daniel 9:25-26; Matthew 27). He exactly met all the descriptions given of Him by the Jewish prophets. And He did the very things the whole volume of inspired Jewish Scriptures foretold concerning Him, mainly, that He would die for our sins, be buried, and be raised again the third day (Psalms 16 and 22; Isaiah 53; 1 Corinthians 15:3-4). If this is not believed and accepted, Jewish people as well as Gentiles must suffer the penalty for their sins, which is eternal separation from God (Isaiah 59:2; Romans 6:23).

The best that the children of Israel could hope for in the Biblical Day of Atonement ritual was to have their sins *atoned for,* covered. Year after year they looked to this solemn day, and if they obeyed the details prescribed for that day, their sins were covered for the past year. Then they went into another year, and again looked to the next Day of Atonement. God could cover their sins because He looked beyond the blood of bullocks and goats and saw the shed blood of His Son. Therefore, God could righteously "pass over" sins done aforetime, that is, ever since Adam. "Being justified freely by His grace through the redemption that is in Christ Jesus: Whom God hath set forth to be a propitiation through faith in His blood, to declare His righteousness for the remission of sins that are past, through the forbearance of God; To declare, I say, at this time His righteousness: that He might be just, and the justifier of him which believeth in Jesus" (Romans 3:24-26; note also Hebrews 9:15).

Note how verse 25 gives the retrospect of Christ's sacrificial death, and how verse 26 gives us the prospect of it. All Jews and Gentiles who believe this glorious gospel are included, for we are "justified freely by His grace through the redemption that is in Christ Jesus." "Neither by the blood of goats and calves, but by His own blood He entered in once into the holy place, having obtained eternal redemption for us. For if the blood of bulls and of goats, and the ashes of an heifer sprinkling the unclean, sanctifieth to the purifying of the flesh: How much more shall the blood of Christ, who through the eternal Spirit offered Himself without spot to God, purge your conscience from dead works to serve the living God?" (Hebrews 9:12-14)

Atonement is really not a New Testament doctrine: it is Old Testament teaching, and part of the old covenant. The word atonement is not even found in the New Testament. In Romans 5:11, the word should be translated *reconciliation* and not *atonement*. This means that the sins of believing individual Jews and Gentiles are not just covered for a year at a time; they are forgiven and forgotten (Hebrews 10:1-18).

Jewish people confess in one of their Day of Atonement prayers that they are exiles from their land because of their sins, and that Messiah alone is their sin-bearer. In this prayer, which I am about to quote, you will be reminded that Messiah, as referred to, is undoubtedly the same suffering Servant of Jehovah spoken of by Isaiah in his remarkable chapter 53, for the language is identical: "Because of our sins we have been exiles from our land and removed far from our native soil, so that we are not able now to do our duty in the house Thou hast chosen, and in the magnificent holy temple upon which Thy name was called, on account of the hand that was stretched out against Thy sanctuary. Our righteous Messiah is departed from us, horror hath seized us, and we have none to justify us. He hath borne the yoke of our transgressions. He beareth our sins on His shoulder that we may find pardon for our iniquities. We shall be healed by His wounds when the Lord creates Him as a new creation. Oh bring Him up from the circle of the earth; raise Him up from Seir to assemble us the second time on Mount Lebanon by the Hand of Yinnon."

The word *Yinnon* refers to the Messiah, so named in the Hebrew text of Psalm 72:17, and affirmed by the Jewish rabbis to be the title of the Messiah. Christ died and thereby made it possible for a Holy God righteously to forgive us our sins. It is for Jew and Gentile to appropriate Him as such.

Both the Feast of Blowing of the Trumpets and this Day of Atonement have a prophetic character. They look forward to a time when Israel will be regathered in their own national homeland, delivered from all their enemies and saved as a nation, as God has promised. This complete regathering and deliverance of the nation will follow the blowing of the heavenly trumpet. Yes, Messiah, the coming Deliverer, will have His Second Advent heralded by trumpet blasts.

In That Day

It is "in that day" that the nation of Israel will afflict her soul and mourn with deep heart affliction. In Zechariah 12 and 13, God tells about this future day of mourning. There we read: "And I will pour upon the house of David, and upon the inhabitants of Jerusalem, the spirit of grace and of supplications: and they shall look upon Me whom they have pierced, and they shall mourn for Him, as one mourneth for his only son, and shall be in bitterness for Him, as one is in bitterness for his firstborn. In that day there shall be great mourning in Jerusalem. . . . In that day there shall be a fountain opened to the house of David and to the inhabitants of Jerusalem for sin and for uncleanness" (Zechariah 12:10-11; 13:1).

This will be the ultimate of all Yom Kippurs; this is the final Day of Atonement. But "in that day" the nation will cease looking to the day and will look to the Person, even her Messiah.

There is something in the original Hebrew text that is most interesting, but not to be found in any of the many versions and translations. Following the word *whom* right in the center of verse 10, there is a Hebrew word of two letters. The letters are the *Aleph* and the *Tau,* the first and last letters of the Hebrew alphabet. The One to whom they will look is the First and the Last, the Beginning and the Ending, the Eternal Son of God. Only He could be the Deliverer out of Zion, who alone can save His people and all who put their trust in Him.

We have the same scene in Revelation 1:4-8. When this Holy One of Israel, speaks through the beloved Apostle John, He says: "I am Alpha and Omega [the first and last letters of the Greek alphabet], the beginning and the ending, saith the Lord, which is, and which was, and which is to come, the Almighty."

"In that day" of Israel's deliverance and salvation as a nation, the remnant that will comprise the nation after two-thirds will have been cut off (Zechariah 13:8-9), will afflict her soul and repent of all her wrong doings, especially in failing to believe in her Messiah, the Christ of God.

Behold the True Atonement

"In that day" the nation will cease to look to a day, even the Day of Atonement, and will look to the Atonement Himself. They will obey Him who spoke through Isaiah: "Look unto Me, and be ye saved, all the ends of the earth: for I am God, and there is none else" (Isaiah 45:22).

Yom Kippur (*Day of Atonement*)

"In that day" the nation will enjoy its greatest victory. It will come through absolute surrender. This will be the Messiah's conquest over them. Man is only free when he is bound to Christ with a chain of love which nothing can sever. When He can cause rebels to surrender and own Him as Lord, then and not until then will they obey and follow Him.

Individual Jews and Gentiles, like Israel "in that day," must surrender before they can triumph and really have victory.

"In that day" there will be intense mourning. But their Deliverer will be present: "To comfort all that mourn; To appoint unto them that mourn in Zion, to give . . . beauty for ashes, the oil of joy for mourning, the garment of praise for the spirit of heaviness."

The redeemed nation will respond: "I will greatly rejoice in the Lord, my soul shall be joyful in my God; for He hath clothed me with the garments of salvation, He hath covered me with the robe of righteousness" (Isaiah 61:2-3, 10).

The individual Jew and Gentile who has "afflicted his soul," i.e., truly repented and trusted the Lord Jesus for salvation, knows something of sorrow for sin. He also knows that:

> He gives me joy in place of sorrow,
> He gives me love that casts out fear:
> He gives me sunshine for my shadow;
> And beauty for ashes here.

"In that day," the nation of Israel will have her sins, not just atoned for, but forgiven, for a fountain will be opened for sin and uncleanness (Zechariah 13:1). That fountain is Calvary—effectively and effectually opened for Israel as a nation.

> There is a fountain filled with blood,
> Drawn from Immanuel's veins,
> And sinners plunged beneath that flood
> Lose all their guilty stains.

"In that day," the prophecy contained in Romans will be gloriously fulfilled: "Blindness in part is happened to Israel, until the fulness of the Gentiles be come in. And so all Israel shall be saved as it is written. There shall come out of Zion the Deliverer, and shall turn away ungodliness from Jacob: For this is My covenant unto them, when I shall take away their sins" (Romans 11:25-27).

And now let us come back to the present. These future things regarding Israel as a nation are interesting and thrilling. But let us consider individual Jews and Gentiles and their need today.

Like Gentiles whose name is Legion, I fear many Jews observe days and neglect realities. These Gentiles I have in mind call themselves Christians, but are simply *professing* Christians, and not true *possessing* Christians. They observe Christmas, for instance, but do not believe in the virgin birth of Christ, nor heed the message of the angel who declared to Jewish shepherds of old: "Behold, I bring you good tidings of great joy, which shall be to all people. For unto you is born this day in the city of David, a Saviour, which is Christ the Lord" (Luke 2:10-11). Some of these people observe Easter Sunday but think not of the resurrection of Christ, nor believe the words of the angel spoken to the women at the empty tomb: "Fear not ye, for I know that ye seek Jesus, which was crucified. He is not here; for He is risen" (Matthew 28). In the same manner I fear there are many Jewish people who observe Yom Kippur, but who do not know any real covering; they have no true atonement for their sins.

Christ's shed blood is the blood of the New Covenant, "Brith Hadasho," spoken by Jeremiah. Read that remarkable chapter 31 of Jeremiah. His sacrificial blood is the only means today by which God can fully forgive us our sins and cleanse us from all unrighteousness.

God grant that many, because of this message, will believe in Him of whom Moses and all the prophets wrote and spoke, even Jeshua of Nazareth. Instead of looking to a day, I beseech you to look to *Him,* Jeshua Hamashiah who is our true Atonement, our only Yom Kippur!

SUCCOTH

Feast of Tabernacles

WE NOW COME to the last of the seven Feasts of Jehovah described in Leviticus 23, the Feast of Tabernacles, known in Jewry today as Succoth. It is also known as the Feast of Ingathering. This joyous holiday follows five days after the solemn Day of Atonement, the only fast day of the seven convocations. It falls on the fifteenth day of Tishri.* The very word Succoth brings happy reminiscences to the Jewish mind. No one but a Jew can appreciate the feelings of joy, contentment, and security that come at the thought of this most happy and satisfying of all the feasts which God gave to the Jewish people. God Himself takes great delight in the glorious future of His people as typified by this happiest of all the celebrations of the Jewish sacred year.

The Feast of Ingathering

"The fifteenth day of this seventh month shall be the feast of tabernacles for seven days unto the Lord. . . . Also in the fifteenth day of the seventh month, when ye have gathered in the fruit of the land, ye shall keep a feast unto the Lord seven days. . . . Ye shall dwell in booths seven days; all that are Israelites born shall dwell in booths: That your generations may know that I made the children of Israel to dwell in booths, when I brought them out of the land of Egypt: I am the Lord

---

*Late September or October.

your God" (Leviticus 23:34, 39, 42, 43).

In Exodus 23, this is called the Feast of Ingathering: "And the feast of harvest, the firstfruits of thy labours, which thou hast sown in the field: and the feast of ingathering, which is in the end of the year, when thou hast gathered in thy labours out of the field" (Exodus 23:16).

If we could transplant ourselves back three thousand years, with Israel back in the land of their fathers, we would see how these instructions were carried out. From the trees, the vines, and the ground itself, the abundance of God's material blessings had been picked, gathered, and brought to the barns and storehouses; and the nation of Israel knew that once more God had provided for them generously for the coming year.

The Feast of Trumpets had come and gone. The terrible days of soul affliction followed, bringing with them deep agony, mortification of soul, repentance and sorrow for sins committed, the plea that God might wipe out the memory of these sins forever, and the solemn reconsecration of the Jewish heart and soul to God, coupled with the vow to live a life more holy and pleasing in His presence. Then came the great Day of Atonement, when upon the scapegoat were placed the sins of the nation, and when, in response to the nation's faith in God, the people of Israel became purged and God could look upon them as a nation whose sins had been atoned for. Then, after the night of sorrow and tears, came the brilliant effulgence of this joyous feast, the Feast of Booths or Tabernacles.

Modern Observance

In commemoration of God's mighty deliverance of His people from Egypt and their forty years of wilderness wandering, when they dwelt in tents and tabernacles, Jewish people today erect booths. In the yards of many homes and adjoining synagogues these booths are erected. During Succoth, meals are eaten in the booth (Succah). In the synagogues, Succoth is observed in a ritual featuring the *lulav* (palm branch), the *esrog* (citron), *shannas* (willow twigs), and *hadassah* (myrtle).

Succoth (Feast of Tabernacles)

The *lulav* and *esrog,* held in the hands of the worshipers, are gently swayed in the direction of the four corners of the earth during the recital of the Hosanna hymns.

Bible Days Observance

In Biblical times one very important and significant ritual of the Feast of Tabernacles was the pouring of water in the Temple. This ceremony lasted seven days. The last day was called *Hosha 'na Rabba,* meaning the *Day of the Great Hosanna.* All of this was done as the priests blew the trumpets. With the waving of their *lulavs,* the Levites and all the people sang the *Great Hallel,* that is, Psalms 113 through 118. Toward the end of the *Hallel* are the words, "Save now, I beseech Thee, O Lord" (Psalm 118:25).

Visualizing this whole scene, it will prove a rich blessing to read these six psalms. Make the words the language of your heart; praise the Lord and rejoice in the goodness of the Lord. Note how Psalm 118 speaks very vividly of the Lord Jesus Christ. This psalm is quoted many times in the New Testament.

The words *save now* in Hebrew are *Hosha 'na Rabba.* So this last day was known as the *Great Hosanna.* All of this throws light on the cry of the people as the Lord Jesus entered Jerusalem just before His crucifixion. The multitude cried out, "Hosanna; Blessed is He that cometh in the name of the Lord . . . Hosanna in the highest" (Mark 11:8-11).

They really cried, 'Save now," but we fear they were also the ones who a few days later cried, "Crucify Him" (Mark 15: 13, 14).

If Any Man Thirst

In the light of these observances, the pouring of water on the last day of the feast, we can understand the significance of what the Lord Jesus said when He attended the Feast of Tabernacles. "Now the Jews' feast of tabernacles was at hand. . . . He [the Lord Jesus] also went up unto the feast. . . . In the last day, that great day of the feast, Jesus stood and cried, saying, If any man thirst, let him come unto Me, and drink. He that believeth on Me, as the scripture [Old Testament Scripture] hath said, out of his belly shall flow rivers of living water. (But this spake He of the Spirit, which they that believe on Him should receive: for the Holy Ghost was not yet given; because Jesus was not yet glorified)" (John 7:2, 10, 37-39).

Prophetic Observance

Now what does this Feast of Tabernacles typify or foretell? Can it mean anything else but that God has revealed in this feast a goal toward which He has been directing all of His marvelously planned program of redemption? Not only redemption of the Jewish nation but through them, eventually, a period of peace for the entire world.

The number seven is very prominent in this Feast of Tabernacles. It is the seventh of the feasts; observed in the seventh month; and was to last seven days. Seven is the Bible number of completion. It was on the seventh day that God rested from all His work of creation (Genesis 2:2). This feast points very definitely to the millennium, considered by many Bible scholars as the seventh dispensation.

It is a feast of rejoicing (Deuteronomy 16:14). Even the land will rejoice in that future day. "The wilderness and the solitary place shall be glad for them; and the desert shall rejoice, and blossom as the rose. It shall blossom abundantly, and rejoice even with joy and singing: the glory of Lebanon shall be given unto it, the excellency of Carmel and Sharon, they shall see the glory of the Lord, and the excellency of our God" (Isaiah 35:1-2).

Jewish people can think back to their childhood days and recall those evensongs that followed the festal Sabbath meals, those heart-touching melodies which expressed the hope that some day the Messiah would come to establish their people once more in their homeland, where they could live in millennial joy for a thousand years that would be "all Sabbath," all

76

peace, quiet, and joy. It was this prophecy contained in the Feast of Tabernacles that those Sabbath songs had in view.

Such is the wonderful future that God still has in store for a redeemed Israel, who will obey and worship Him with sincerity of heart. Of that day Zechariah tells us: "Thus saith the Lord of hosts; in those days it shall come to pass, that ten men shall take hold out of all languages of the nations, even shall take hold of the skirt of him that is a Jew, saying, We will go with you: for we have heard that God is with you" (Zechariah 8:23).

Whither Thou Goest I Will Go

This means that the Gentile peoples of the world will come to the spiritually reborn people of Israel and say to them in effect, "Please show us the way to God." It will be much like that which the Moabite girl, Ruth, said to her Jewish mother-in-law, Naomi: "For whither thou goest, I will go; and where thou lodgest, I will lodge: thy people shall be my people, and thy God my God: Where thou diest, will I die, and there will I be buried" (Ruth 1:16-17).

And so in this sense, the Feast of Tabernacles will also be the Feast of Ingathering. For as the Feast of Tabernacles was meant to celebrate each year the harvest of the land, so in that blessed era known as the millennium, the world will witness the gathering of all the nations to the Messiah. Even though the gathering of many peoples to Him has already been going on for centuries, as Jacob prophesied, "Unto Him shall the gathering of the people be" (Genesis 49:10), yet at that time *all the nations shall flow* unto Him. It will be a truly great Feast of Ingathering.

At the beginning of that wonderful millennial era of Tabernacles, the Jewish people, purified through tribulation sufferings, will look to King Messiah who will return to earth. He will bring about a miraculous deliverance, both physically and spiritually. As foretold by both Old and New Testament prophets, the Jewish nation in that future day will be saved by looking to Him, the One who was pierced on God's altar of sacrifice 1,900 years ago.

This will be the beginning, the entrance door to the blessed age to come. The nation of Israel will repent of the great mistake made when Messiah came the first time, in fulfillment of the Jewish Scriptures, and died for our sins. Israel as a nation rejected Him then, but in this future day the nation of Israel will turn to Him and be born again, for they will call upon the name of the Lord (Romans 10:13). "They shall call upon My name, and I will hear them [saith the Lord]: I will say, It is My people: and they shall say, The Lord is my God" (Zechariah 13:9).

The Future Feast of Tabernacles

Again God describes to us the glory and splendor of that great Feast of Tabernacles to come: "And it shall be in that day, that living waters shall go out from Jerusalem; half of them toward the former sea, and half of them toward the hinder sea: in summer and in winter shall it be. And the Lord shall be king over all the earth: in that day shall there be one Lord, and His name one. . . . And men shall dwell in it, and there shall be no more utter destruction; but Jerusalem shall be safely inhabited. . . . And it shall come to pass, that every one that is left of all the nations which came against Jerusalem shall even go up from year to year to worship the King, the Lord of hosts, and to keep the feast of tabernacles" (Zechariah 14: 8-16).

What a remarkable prophecy this is. And to know that it will be literally fulfilled to the letter! What destruction has been wrought these past terrible years, and what utter destruction will yet take place before Messiah comes back in fulfillment of Zechariah's prophecy; but a day will dawn when those shadows will all flee away.

The True Succoth, a Person

Is there a place of safety and security for individuals to-

Succoth (Feast of Tabernacles)

day? There is such a place for individual Jews and Gentiles in this year of our Lord. The very joys and blessings that God has prepared for the world, in that great day of the Feast of Tabernacles, can be possessed by individual Jews and Gentiles now. Will the United Nations Organization bring us into this place of safety and security? Will the threat of a devastating nuclear war do it? No, our only escape from the wrath to come, and our hope of Heaven are not in the counsels of men. Our hope is in the Lord God. We are not to look to a power, but to a Person. That person is Jeshua of Nazareth, the true Messiah who came 1,900 years ago and offered Himself a sacrifice for our sins. That place outside the city wall of Jerusalem where our Lord, the Saviour Messiah, shed His precious blood, is the only place of mercy and security and safety. He, God's spotless Lamb, died for our sins and rose again according to the Old Testament Scriptures. He is our Succoth, our Booth, our True Tabernacle. How I praise God that He built a Succoth for us, and provided Himself the sacrifice in fulfillment of the Jewish Scriptures. Believing Jews and Gentiles dwell in Him, our Tabernacle, the only true and safe Succoth today.

We should keep *the* Succoth, the one that God ordained for our days. God has built a Succoth, and provided the sacrifice for cleansing. The Jewish Messiah is our Succoth, our Tabernacle. He is even called that in the book of Amos. There we read that He is coming again to establish the throne of David: "In that day will I raise up the tabernacle [Succoth] of David that is fallen" (Amos 9:11).

The same statement is found in the New Testament (Acts 15:15-16).

His soul was made an offering for sin (Isaiah 53:10). The Messiah's death was the supreme sacrifice and in His death He fulfilled all the Old Testament types and pictures of Himself. Now He is the sacrifice needed for cleansing. When He came 1,900 years ago, He fulfilled the prophetic statement made by Himself through King David: "Sacrifice and offering Thou dost not desire; mine ears hast Thou opened: burnt-offering and sin-offering hast Thou not required. Then said I, Lo, I come: in the volume of the book it is written of Me" (Psalm 40:6-7; Hebrews 10:5-18).

The speaker of these words is the Messiah. When the sacrifices of the Old Covenant were abolished, the Messiah of the New Covenant came to take their place, according to the plan and promise of God (Jeremiah 31:33). No feast or holy occasion is complete or acceptable to God without the Messiah. He sanctifies all our feasts, because His blood cleanses from sin. He is the Lamb of God which taketh away the sin of the world (Isaiah 53:7; John 1:29).

If we refuse Him who speaks to us (Hebrews 12:25), or neglect His great salvation (Hebrews 2:1-3), the night will come when our hearts will cry out: "The harvest is past, the summer is ended, and we are not saved" (Jeremiah 8:20).

How good to know that today there is balm in Gilead; the Great Physician is here to save and cleanse from all sin.

If we simply believe the record that God gave of His Son, the true Succoth, and receive Him as our Saviour-Messiah, we will have the Feast of Tabernacles in our hearts and souls today (John 1:12-13:1 John 5:10-13). That will be far better than these two days of celebrating, for that will last through time and throughout eternity. Behold Him, Jeshuah Hamashiah, your true Succoth. Believe in Him and abide in Him forever.

HANUKKAH

Feast of Lights

HANUKKAH is another happy, festive, joyous day in Jewry. It falls on Kislev 25 according to the Jewish calendar.* It symbolizes freedom from oppression.

I would like to be in that fast-growing, beautiful city of Jerusalem these days. On Christmas Eve, with hundreds of others from all over the world, I would go down to that little town of Bethlehem over in Jordan, spend the night there, so as to be in that old Biblical city on Christmas morn. If I were in Jerusalem during this week of festivities, I would enter the Yeshuron, the stately synagogue on Karen Street; and with head covered, I would celebrate Hanukkah with hundreds of Jewish people gathered in that beautiful building. Of course, I would remember to bring my *yamulka* (scull cap) and *tallith* (prayer shawl) to conform properly to custom.

This eight-day festive season commemorates the Jewish victory over the demoralizing and oppressing Syrians and ancient Greeks, who aimed to eradicate Judaism. The revolt against Antiochus Epiphanes, the enemy of the Jews, was started by an old priest, named Mattathias of Modin, and it continued under his brave son, Judas Maccabaeus. On the twenty-fifth of the month Kislev (B.C. 164), three years after the Temple had been so blasphemously defiled, Judas Maccabaeus with a small army of Jewish soldiers victoriously entered

---

*Kislev coincides with December.

Jerusalem, cleansed and repaired and rededicated the Temple.

It would seem that this was in fulfillment of Daniel's prophecy found in Daniel 9:9-12. At least most Bible scholars so teach. Perhaps what happened in B.C. 164 was a near fulfillment and the far or complete fulfillment will take place during the time of Jacob's trouble (Jeremiah 30:6-8), referred to by the Lord Messiah as the great tribulation (Matthew 24: 15-22).

Hanukkah celebration lasts eight days. On the first day the *shammash,* the prominent branch of the *Hanukkah Menorah,* the nine-branched candlestick, is lighted. The *shammash,* which means *servant,* is usually in the center and is the tallest of the branches of the candlestick. From it each of the other branches is lighted on subsequent days, until all are lighted.

Tradition tells us that one of the priests in B.C. 164 found a cruse of unpolluted oil. With this the candlestick was replenished. It is also said that this small quantity of oil was miraculously increased so that it lasted eight days. Hence, the eight days of festivities.

The way in which Jewish people celebrate Hanukkah today is very significant. The customs of this joyous season point very definitely to the One of whom all the divinely inspired Jewish prophets of old wrote, the One revealed in the New Testament.

Israeli Torchbearers

One of the very interesting and exciting customs in Israel during this historic celebration is the carrying of the Hanukkah Torch of Freedom from Modin to Jerusalem. The torches are lighted in Modin, the historic site near Lydda, where the Maccabees rebelled in ancient times. The flaming spears are carried by marathon runners, both young men and women. They run from Modin in relays to Tel Aviv and then on to Jerusalem, where torchlight processions are held.

Hanukkah (Feast of Lights)

Hanukkah and Christmas

In many ways the Jewish Hanukkah celebration is similar to Christmas. Both were originated in the same land by the same people. Both occur on the same day of their respective months; twenty-fifth Kislev and twenty-fifth of December. On both holidays gifts are exchanged. In the celebrations special songs are sung: "Mo' Oz Tzur" (Rock of My Salvation) on Hanukkah, and carols during the Christmas season. Both are in commemoration of great historic events that changed the whole cause of mankind. Lights are the order of the day for both Hanukkah and Christmas. In both observances the Servant has the place of prominence; the *Shammash* (meaning *servant*), the ninth branch of the Menorah; and the Messiah, the Suffering Servant of Jehovah. Both observances are highly commercialized. To quote from a Jewish newspaper (*The National Jewish Post,* December 16, 1960), "The biggest Jewish show in America today is the Annual Hanukkah Festival, staged under the auspices of Israel Bonds." And all know what a great stimulus Christmas is to business.

First-Century Hanukkah

This happy festival is not mentioned in the Old Testament for the simple reason that the historic event occurred during the four-hundred-year period between the two Testaments. It is mentioned, however, in the New Testament: "And it was at Jerusalem the feast of the dedication, and it was winter" (John 10:22). Here it is called the Feast of Dedication. *Hanukkah* in Hebrew means *dedication*. It is spoken of as the Feast of Lights today.

Back in B.C. 164, the question arose as to what should be done with the old desecrated altar upon which a sow had been sacrificed. It was decided to pull down and store the stones of it in a convenient place, "until there should come a prophet to give an answer concerning them" (1 Maccabees 4: 44-46). About two centuries later, on the anniversary of this

83

event, the Messiah was in the Temple courts, no doubt celebrating Hanukkah with His fellow Jews. Recognizing that He, Jesus of Nazareth, was a great Prophet, they remembered the question raised years before about the Temple stones. He gave the answer, not merely about the stones of the desecrated altar, but concerning *the* Stone (Genesis 49:24; Psalm 118:22; Acts 4:11-12): "And it was at Jerusalem the feast of dedication, and it was winter. And Jesus walked in the temple in Solomon's porch. Then came the Jews round about Him, and said unto Him, How long dost Thou make us to doubt? If Thou be the Christ, tell us plainly (John 10:22-24).

This was the appropriate time for them to ask this question, for it was during the celebration of Israel's national deliverance, during the days of the Maccabees. In language that could not be misunderstood, He claimed to be a greater Maccabee (Hammerer); One who would bring about a deliverance not only for time, but for eternity: He claimed to be "that Prophet" who was to come (Deuteronomy 18:15-19; Acts 7:37), even the promised Messiah (John 4:25-26), the Son of God (John 10:29-30).

The True Light

I mentioned eight points wherein both Hanukkah and Christmas are similar. Both originated in the same land by the same people; both on the twenty-fifth of the month; gifts exchanged; special songs sung; commemoration of great historic events; lights; prominence of Servant; and commercialization. As this is known as the Feast of Lights, we will consider only this sixth similarity, Lights.

The true Shammash, the Servant of Jehovah said: "I am the light of the world: he that followeth Me shall not walk in darkness, but shall have the light of life" (John 8:12).

Just as the *Shammash* on the Hanukkah Memorah lights all the other branches, Christ is the true Light who gives light to all who come in contact with Him, all who believe in Him.

Hanukkah (Feast of Lights)

"This is the condemnation, that light is come into the world, and men loved darkness rather than light, because their deeds were evil. For every one that doeth evil hateth the light, neither cometh to the light, lest his deeds should be reproved. But he that doeth truth cometh to the light, that his deeds may be made manifest, that they are wrought in God" (John 3:19-21).

To His brethren after the flesh, He cries out: "Arise, shine; for thy light is come, and the glory of the Lord is risen upon thee. For, behold, the darkness shall cover the earth, and gross darkness the people: but the Lord shall arise upon thee, and His glory shall be seen upon thee. And the Gentiles shall come to thy light, and kings to the brightness of thy rising" (Isaiah 60:1-3). "A light to lighten the Gentiles, and the glory of Thy people Israel" (Luke 2:32).

Light dispels darkness. Light enables people to see. Light brings life. Light purifies. Light heals. "The Lord is my light and my salvation" (Psalm 27:1).

He is the effulgence of God's glory (Hebrews 1:3). For any who are in darkness to these spiritual truths, this message is given: "To open their eyes, and to turn them from darkness to light, and from the power of Satan unto God, that they may receive forgiveness of sins, and inheritance among them which are sanctified by faith that is in Me [Christ]" (Acts 26:18).

A few years ago, in New York City, I was visiting a Jewish man who had been listening to our Message to Israel broadcasts. He had been reading the Old Testament Prophecy Edition of the New Testament that I had sent to him. In response to my questioning him as to his belief, he said, "Mr. Shepherd, now I see; I see that Jesus is our Messiah, the Son of God. He must be, for He came the very time our Moses said He would come (Genesis 49:10), and He came of the very tribe that Moses foretold (Genesis 49:8, 9). He came the very way our great Isaiah said He would come, by way of the virgin's womb (Isaiah 7:14), and He was born in the very city our Micah predicted, Bethlehem (Micah 5:2). Yes, and

85

now I see He is the One of whom our Isaiah wrote in his fifty-third chapter."

His eyes were opened so that he could see these truths. How were they opened? He came to the Light; he believed in Jeshua and confessed Him as Lord; he believed in his heart that Jesus died for his sins and rose again according to the Old Testament Scriptures (1 Corinthians 15:1-4). Because he came to the Light, darkness was dispelled; he could see; he had life; he was cleansed from all sin.

An Eternal Bright City

The Scripture tells of an Eternal City, where all Jewish and Gentile believers will dwell forever with their Saviour: "And the city had no need of the sun, neither of the moon, to shine in it: for the glory of God . . . is the light thereof. And the nations of them which are saved shall walk in the light of it . . . for there shall be no night there" (Revelation 21:23-25). "I Jesus . . . am the root and the offspring of David, and the bright and morning star" (Revelation 22:16).

It was a great deliverance that God wrought through the Maccabees over 2,100 years ago. But here is a greater victory. The Lord Jesus Christ defeated the powers of darkness. There is deliverance from sin for Jews and Gentiles who believe in Him as the true light and the world's only Saviour.

God grant that He might illuminate darkened minds and hearts. He will do this for those who will make Him their true Hanukkah today. He will deliver from the penalty of sin, from the power and practice of sin, and one day from the very presence of sin (1 Corinthians 9:24-28).

> Come to the Light, 'tis shining for thee;
> Sweetly the light has dawned upon me;
> Once I was blind, but now I can see:
> The Light of the world is Jesus.

CHRISTMAS

Birth of the Messiah

SHOULD CHRISTMAS be considered a Jewish holiday? Whose birth is celebrated during this happy season? The Messiah of Israel! The prophecies concerning the birth of this Holy One of Israel are found in the Old Testament Scriptures. The record of His birth is found in the New Testament Scriptures, which are also Jewish. The forty writers of sacred Scripture were holy Jewish men of God. They all wrote and spoke of the Messiah. In the volume of the whole Jewish Book it is written of Him (Psalm 40:7; Hebrews 10:7).

It was Jewish shepherds who were startled years ago in old Bethlehem by a message that completely changed their lives, and that has reverberated down through the halls of time: "And there were in the same country shepherds abiding in the field, keeping watch over their flock by night. And, lo, the angel of the Lord came upon them, and the glory of the Lord shone round about them: and they were sore afraid. And the angel said unto them, Fear not: for, behold, I bring you good tidings of great joy, which shall be to all people. For unto you is born this day in the city of David a Saviour, which is Christ the Lord" (Luke 2:8-11).

It was Jewish shepherds who first believed in Him and who proclaimed the message of salvation. It was Jewish men who became His followers, His disciples. It was Jewish people who comprised the Church in the very beginning.

Jewish Holy Days

Christmas Brings Blessings

In many places and in many ways Jewish people today receive great benefits from Christmas. Christmas is the greatest stimulus to business the storekeeper has. In most cities all around the world the great department stores and lesser shops are owned by Jewish people. Do away with Christmas and depression would follow in that void.

Christmas brings blessings to all peoples. The promise of God to Abraham, "In thee shall all families of the earth be blessed" (Genesis 12:3), becomes alive at Christmas. Where the birth of the Jewish Messiah is not celebrated, there is no real blessing, no joy, no benefit for today, no hope for tomorrow.

Christmas knows no barriers and recognizes no bounds. It benefits all peoples, all races, all colors, rich or poor, firm or infirm. Jewish people especially should lift their hearts in gratitude to God, the God of Abraham, Isaac, and Jacob, that the Hope of Israel was finally manifested in flesh. The longing, the hope, the faith of the Jewish fathers, kings, and prophets were at last realized when the Word of Promise became flesh. Moses, Isaiah, Micah, and all the prophets wrote of Him: "His hands were made strong by the hands of the mighty God of Jacob; (from thence is the shepherd, the stone of Israel)" (Genesis 49:24). "Therefore the Lord Himself shall give you a sign; Behold, a virgin shall conceive, and bear a son, and shall call His name Immanuel" (Isaiah 7:14). "For unto us a child is born, unto us a son is given" (Isaiah 9:6). "But thou, Bethlehem Ephratah, though thou be little among the thousands of Judah, yet out of thee shall He come forth unto Me that is to be ruler in Israel; whose goings forth have been from of old, from everlasting" (Micah 5:2).

If we receive only material blessings and benefits through Christmas, we miss the true meaning of the season, and lose out eternally. These material benefits are transitory and temporal. The greatest blessing is reserved for those who believe in the One whose birth is celebrated at this season. We are ex-

88

horted to "Look not at the things which are seen, but at the things which are not seen: for the things which are seen are temporal; but the things which are not seen are eternal" (2 Corinthians 4:18).

The Date of Birth

Many people object to the name Christmas and refuse to join in any festivities on December 25, because in all probability Christ was not born on that date. The very name "Christmas," however, is the confession of belief in the incarnation of the Son of God, for the word means "Christ-sent." For Him to be sent presupposes His pre-existence.

It is quite evident that the Lord Jesus was not born on December 25. Yet it is a well-known fact that early Christians, including Hebrew Christians, observed this date as a special day as far back as A.D. 98. Clement of Alexandria, at the very beginning of the third century, records the keeping of this date.

The *birth* of Christ was not the miracle. The angels announced the *begetting*. The great emphasis is placed in Scripture upon the *conception*. That was the miracle. The correct rendering of Matthew 1:18 is: "Now the *genesis* of Jesus Christ was on this wise." The inspired writer is showing that Jesus was *conceived* in a different way than all others in His genealogy, as well as all human beings who have ever come into the world.

It has been fairly well established that December 25 is the date of *conception*. The perfect period of human gestation is 280 days. That would make September 29 the date of the birth of the Son of God. If this is correct, in all probability the Messiah of Israel was born about the time of the Feast of Tabernacles: perhaps on the very date, Tishri 15! "The word was made flesh, and dwelt [tabernacled] among us" (John 1:14). The Feast of Tabernacles fittingly symbolizes the dwelling of God among men.

In any event, the date is not important; but the fact that Christ was born of a virgin in the city of Bethlehem is all-important. To ignore or doubt this fact disqualifies a person for salvation, whether he be Jew or Gentile.

The Romance of the Incarnation

"Now the birth of Jesus Christ was on this wise: When as His mother Mary was espoused to Joseph, before they came together, she was found with child of the Holy Ghost. Then Joseph her husband, being a just man, and not willing to make her a public example, was minded to put her away privily" (Matthew 1:18-19).

Let us stop and consider these two godly young people, Mary and Joseph. This young Jewess and her fiancé were both descendants of David: one through David's son Nathan; the other, Joseph, through his son, Solomon.

Think first about Mary: as told in the Gospel of Luke, chapter 1, God dealt very graciously with her. He sent an angel and announced to her—His chosen vessel—that before her marriage, before she lived with her husband Joseph, while she was still a virgin, she was to have a child, and that child would be a son. Because of the delicacy of this story, we cannot go into detail. But suffice it to say, Mary was confronted with a situation that no other maiden ever faced. If she agreed to be the channel through whom the Messiah was to come, she would encounter an unprecedented position.

According to God's holy law, under which her people lived, she would be stoned to death. But suppose she would be willing to let God have His way with her, and ignore public opinion. "What about my godly father?" she thought. "It will break his heart; it will bring a blot upon the family name. He will not understand this. What will he think and what will he do about this? And my precious tender-souled mother: she could not survive the shock. I could not make her believe it. An untimely grave would be hers and I would be the cause of it." So thought Mary. "And if I should not consider my father and mother, what about my lover?" she reasoned within herself. "My lover, dear good Joseph, that fine righteous and holy man! What will he say and do about it? Life without him now would not be worth living!"

Can you not picture this beautiful, godly young Jewess thus reasoning? I seem to see her throw up her hands in full surrender to the will of God, bow her head, and with a yielded heart cry out, *"Behold the handmaid of the Lord; be it unto me according to Thy word!"* (Luke 1:38) "Cost what it may, Oh God, Thy will be done in me!"

Now consider Joseph. He loved Mary, his espoused wife. He knew she was with child, and that he was not the father. His heart was broken. God tells us he was a just man, a righteous man, and that he was not willing to make her a public example. His desire was to be true to his promise, but he dare not carry out the engagement that would make her his wife. He reasoned within himself how he could put her away privately. He was trying to find ways and means of breaking the engagement without making her a public example.

Now God knew Joseph's heart and "While he thought on these things, behold, the angel of the Lord appeared unto him in a dream, saying, Joseph, thou son of David, fear not to take unto thee Mary thy wife: for that which is conceived in her is of the Holy Ghost. And she shall bring forth a son, and thou shalt call His name JESUS: for He shall save His people from their sins. Now all this was done, that it might be fulfilled which was spoken of the Lord by the prophet, saying, Behold, a virgin shall be with child, and shall bring forth a son, and they shall call His name Emmanuel, which being interpreted is, God with us. Then Joseph being raised from sleep did as the angel of the Lord had bidden him, and took unto him his wife: And knew her not till she had brought forth her firstborn son: and he called His name JESUS. Now . . . Jesus was born in Bethlehem of Judea" (Matthew 1:20-2:1).

In this divinely inspired account of the birth of the Messiah, we see the romance of the incarnation.

Born According to Scripture

Consider just a few of the prophecies that were fulfilled at Christ's birth:

1. He was to be the seed of the woman. Every other person ever born is the seed of the male (Genesis 3:15; Galatians 3:16).

2. He was to be born at a specific time in history (Genesis 49:10).

3. He was to come from the tribe of Judah (Genesis 49:10; Hebrews 7:14).

4. He was to be the Son of Abraham and the Son of David (2 Samuel 7:12; Matthew 1:1).

5. He was to be called the Son of God (Psalm 2:7; Isaiah 9:6; Proverbs 30:4; Luke 1:32).

6. He was to be born of a virgin. That is the only way He could be the seed of the woman (Isaiah 7:14; Matthew 1:18-23).

7. His name was to be called Immanuel (Isaiah 7:14; Matthew 1:23).

8. He was to be born in Bethlehem (Micah 5:2; Matthew 2:1).

Whence Art Thou?

Pilate asked the question of Jesus, "Whence art Thou?" (John 19:9) The whole Word of God answers that question. He is pictured in Psalm 8 as One who for a little while was made lower than Elohim, for that is the correct rendering of verse 5. Elohim, the plural name by which we are first introduced to God (Genesis 1:1). God, the strong One: *El* is singular and *Elohim* is plural. The Lord Jesus is seen in this uni-plural name. In the beginning was the triune God. "And God said, Let *Us* make man in *Our* image, after *Our* likeness. . . ." (Genesis 1:26).

The great Creator became our Saviour. The second Person of the Godhead stepped down from that excellent glory and "made Himself of no reputation, and took upon Him the form of a servant, and was made in the likeness of men: And being found in fashion as a man, He humbled Himself, and became obedient unto death, even the death of the cross. Wherefore God also hath highly exalted Him, and given Him a name which is above every name" (Philippians 2:6-9).

The book of Hebrews is the commentary on the eighth Psalm. We have a right to read the commentary to conform with the correct rendering of the verse quoted in Psalm 8: "We see Jesus, who for a little while was made lower than Elohim, for the suffering of death, crowned with glory and honor; that he by the grace of God should taste death for every man" (Hebrews 2:9).

Born to Die

The Messiah was born that He might die for our sins. He gave Himself a sacrifice for the sins of every person. That is why He said: "I lay down my life, that I might take it again. No man taketh it from Me, but I lay it down Myself. I have power to lay it down, and I have power to take it again" (John 10:17-18). He delivered up His own Spirit, and only God can do that (John 19:30, 33).

Whose birth is being celebrated during the Christmas season? The Messiah of Israel, the great Creator, God manifest as a man. The Second Person of the trinity became a man that He might die. "He hath appeared to put away sin by the sacrifice of Himself" (Hebrews 9:26). "And ye know that He was manifested to take away our sins; and in Him is no sin" (1 John 3:5).

Heart belief in the Person of Christ and the work of Christ is absolutely essential to salvation. A Saviour who is not quite God is like a bridge broken down at the far end. The God-Man must die (John 3:14) for our sins. He must shed His precious blood so that a holy God can righteously forgive all the sins of those who fully trust Him (Leviticus 17:11; Matthew 26:28). This is the fundamental of all fundamentals. One must believe in the Person and work of the Christ of God, as revealed in the Scriptures, to be saved from his sins.

During World War I when American G.I.'s were locked in a battle to the death, a miracle took place. It was Christmas and someone shouted, "Today is Christmas!" That shout echoed and reechoed throughout the trenches on both sides. That magic word electrified the atmosphere. American and German soldiers climbed over the top and enemies became friends in "No Man's Land." In the spirit of that magic word, *Christmas,* the enmity between the two forces was dispelled. American and German soldiers fraternized with one another. Why? All because a Babe was born 1,900 years ago.

This instance is a foretaste, an earnest of the peace that will reign when the Prince of Peace Himself comes back to earth. Then the anthem sung by the heavenly choir 1,900 years ago will be literally true: "Glory to God in the highest, and on earth peace, good will toward men" (Luke 2:13-14).

Messiah Could Not Be Born Today

Some of our orthodox Jewish friends believe the Messiah will come any day in fulfillment of the Messianic hope. Is it possible for Him to be born today?

No, because He must come from the seed of Abraham, from the house of David, and from the Tribe of Judah (Genesis 11:10-32; 49:8-10; 2 Samuel 7:12-14). Since the destruction of the Temple in A.D. 70, all authentic genealogies (of genuine origin) respecting the twelve tribes of Israel have been lost. No one today could prove his identity authentically.

No, because He must die by crucifixion according to Psalm 22. That mode of capital punishment is not practiced today in Israel or any place in the Middle East.

No, because He already came over 1,900 years ago, according to all Scripture and history. "The fulness of time was come [1,900 years ago], God sent forth His Son, made of a woman, made under the law, to redeem them that were under the law" (Galatians 4:4-5).

Christmas (*Birth of Messiah*)

Born in Hearts

"He came unto His own, and His own received Him not. But as many as received Him, to them gave He power to become the sons of God, even to them that believe on His name: Which were born, not of blood, nor of the will of the flesh, nor of the will of man, but of God." (John 1:11-13).

Hark! The herald angels sing,
  "Glory to the newborn King;
Peace on earth, and mercy mild;
  God and sinners reconciled."
Joyful, all ye nations, rise,
  Join the triumph of the skies;
With angelic hosts proclaim,
  "Christ is born in Bethlehem."

Christ, by highest Heaven adored;
  Christ, the everlasting Lord;
Late in time behold Him come,
  Offspring of a virgin's womb,
Veiled in flesh the Godhead see,
  Hail the Incarnate Deity!
Pleased as man with men to dwell,
  Jesus, our Immanuel.

Hail the Heaven-born Prince of Peace!
  Hail the Son of righteousness!
Light and life to all He brings,
  Risen with healing in His wings:
Mild He lays His glory by;
  Born that man no more may die;
Born to raise the sons of earth;
  Born to give them second birth.

CHARLES WESLEY